Other Telecom Titles From Aegis Publishing Group

Winning Communications Strategies:
How Small Businesses Master Cutting-Edge Technology to Stay Competitive, Provide Better Service and Make More Money
by Jeffrey Kagan
$14.95   0-9632790-8-4

Getting the Most From Your Yellow Pages Advertising
by Barry Maher
$19.95   1-890154-05-9

Telecom Glossary:
Understanding Telecommunications Technology
$9.95   1-890154-02-4

Telecom Made Easy:
Money-Saving, Profit-Building Solutions for Home Businesses, Telecommuters and Small Organizations, by June Langhoff
$19.95   0-9632790-7-6

The Telecommuter's Advisor:
Working in the Fast Lane, by June Langhoff
$14.95   0-9632790-5-X

900 Know-How:
How to Succeed With Your Own 900 Number Business
by Robert Mastin
$19.95   0-9632790-3-3

The Business Traveler's Survival Guide:
How to Get Work Done While on the Road, by June Langhoff
$9.95   1-890154-03-2

Phone Company Services
Working Smarter With the Right Telecom Tools, by June Langhoff
$9.95   1-890154-01-6

Money-Making 900 Numbers:
How Entrepreneurs Use the Telephone to Sell Information
by Carol Morse Ginsburg and Robert Mastin
$19.95   0-9632790-1-7

Telecom Business Opportunities

*The Entrepreneur's Guide
to Making Money in the
Telecommunications Revolution*

Steve Rosenbush

Aegis Publishing Group, Ltd.
796 Aquidneck Avenue
Newport, Rhode Island 02842
401-849-4200
www.aegisbooks.com

Library of Congress Catalog Card Number: 97-73916

International Standard Book Number: 1-890154-04-0

Printed in the United States of America.

10 9 8 7 6 5 4 3 2 1

This publication is designed to provide accurate and authoritative information in regard to the subject matter covered. It is sold with the understanding that neither the author nor the publisher is engaged in rendering legal, accounting, or other professional service. If legal advice or other expert assistance is required, the services of a competent professional should be sought.

Publisher's Cataloging In Publication Data
Rosenbush, Steve
Telecom Business Opportunities: The Entrepreneur's Guide to Making Money in the Telecommunications Revolution / by Steve Rosenbush.
1. Telecommunications.
TK5101.R68   1998   384   97-73916

ISBN 1-890154-04-0

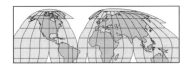

Acknowldgements

A great many people contributed to this book, directly and indirectly. Many of those contributions are obvious in the following pages. The entrepreneurs, executives, analysts, and investors who shared their insights and experiences with me are too numerous to mention here, but they should know how much I appreciate their generosity. I really couldn't have finished this project without them. I will mention a few names, though, at the risk of offending everyone else. Jeff Kagan of Kagan Telecom Associates deserves a special thanks. So does Todd Lowe of Visiology Inc., who shared an enormous amount of time and data. Thanks to my publisher Bob Mastin, for his patience and enthusiasm, and to my editor, Francis "Nim" Marsh, for all his careful work, and to Jonathan Pillot, for all his advice. Thanks to the newspaper editors who have supported me, too: Roz Liston of United Press International, Dave Allen of *The Star-Ledger*; and Geri Tucker of *USA Today*. Thanks to Judith Stein, the former head of the English Department at Kenwood Academy in Chicago. Profound thanks to my parents, Martin and Donna Rosenbush, who spent many hours tutoring a six-year-old in their living room and thereby shaped a life. My wife Dori spent a great deal of time reading rough drafts, sounding out ideas, keeping me motivated, and doing the laundry when it was really my turn. Thanks most of all to her and our daughter Amira, who put up with my long hours and cheered me up.

For Dori and Amira

Contents

Strategy and Management

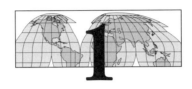

Bell Telephone vs. Western Union

The Entrepreneur in Telecommunications History

During its great periods of upheaval, the telecommunications market has always belonged to the entrepreneur. It's been that way since the invention of the telephone itself. The telephone was created in one of history's great feats of entrepreneurship. A 29-year-old inventor named Alexander Graham Bell was among a handful of researchers attempting to solve one of the great technological problems of 1876: how to transmit the sound of a human voice over a copper wire.

These researchers were dismissed as dreamers in a world in which the Pony Express still drove teams of horses across the American prairie to deliver the mail. The state of the art in communications was the telegraph, which converted coded messages into electrical impulses and sent them over copper wires to distant receivers, where operators decoded the impulses into short written messages.

Alexander Graham Bell, 1876.

Property of AT&T Archives. Reprinted with permission of AT&T.

Bell envisioned something revolutionary: a new type of network that would allow people in distant cities or even distant countries to converse as though they were in the same room. Such a system would obliterate the delays and limitations of Morse code and brief written messages. It would allow instantaneous, natural communications across great distance for the first time in history. It would be the beginning of modern communications.

Bell obtained a patent for the telephone on March 7, 1876, stating that he had succeeded in transmitting some voice sounds, albeit unintelligible ones, over a wire. A competitor, Elisha Grey, filed a caveat with the patent office two hours later, announcing that he was working on the same problem. Three days later Bell succeeded in transmitting the first intelligible voice sounds over his telephone: "Mr. Watson, come here, I want you."

But Bell was no businessman, according to AT&T archivist Sheldon Hochheiser. He was devoted to research, and he supported himself by teaching classes for deaf children. The fathers of two of Bell's students were excited by his research and agreed to help him develop his ideas. Thus, Gardiner Hubbard and Thomas Sanders funded Bell's research and provided the seed money for a start-up venture launched in 1877 in Boston, known as the Bell Telephone Co., to manufacture telephones. The following year New England Telephone was established to provide telephone service to the region, and the company agreed to lease all its phones from Bell Telephone.

Investors weren't flocking to the company, though. Hungry for cash, Hubbard offered to sell the telephone patent to Western Union for $100,000 in the winter of 1877. The world seemed comfortably in Western Union's grasp as William Orton surveyed it from his office at company headquarters in New York City. The company was among the first great modern corporations, larger and more powerful than all but a few railroads. So it's understandable, perhaps, that Orton regarded the telephone as an electrical toy. His judgment may have been clouded, too, by a long-standing conflict with Hubbard, who had been a leading advocate of a federal telegraph network that would have rivaled Western Union. Orton dismissed Hubbard's offer and let one of the great opportunities in history slip by.

Hubbard, a prominent patent attorney, was the business

Gardiner Greene Hubbard, Boston attorney, who became Alexander Graham Bell's father-in-law and the first business manager of the telephone system.

Property of AT&T Archives. Reprinted with permission of AT&T.

leader of the nascent company. As he struggled to bring Bell's ideas to market, he drew upon his experience with an earlier venture. He had once financed a company that made equipment for shoe manufacturers. The company defrayed its capital costs by licensing the technology to other businessmen. Using a similar model, Hubbard licensed Bell's technology to other carriers who carved out Bell Telephone territories for themselves. Bell Telephone further maintained

Thomas Sanders, who backed the telephone to the extent of $110,000 before it brought him any return.

Property of AT&T Archives. Reprinted with permission of AT&T.

control of the telephone instruments and leased them to its regional operators.

Bell Telephone began commercial operations in 1877 by providing private lines that could be used only for calls between two fixed points. Shortly thereafter, in 1878, the first network switch was installed at New Haven, Connecticut, allowing customers to converse with other people who were connected to the same local exchange. By then stock traders who conducted their business over Western Union telegraph wires were suddenly demanding telephone lines from the company. Orton realized that his first impression of the telephone was mistaken, and he scrambled to reverse course. Western Union bought Elisha Grey's patent rights, launched the American Speaking Telephone Company, and engaged light bulb inventor Thomas Edison to refine the telephone. Bell Telephone sued for patent infringement and a settlement was reached in 1879. It was clear that Orton still didn't understand the profound changes that were underway in the world of communications. Western Union left the telephone network business in exchange for royalties on every phone Bell Telephone sold. In return, Bell Telephone agreed to leave the telegraph business. The settlement only made Western Union's troubles worse.

Orton had sealed the company's fate with a single, irreversible bad decision. The telephone was changing human communications; Western Union had been offered one chance to lead that change, and it wouldn't get another. Orton had set his great corporation on a downward spiral that would culminate with a trip to bankruptcy court in the next century. As for Bell Telephone: It would evolve into AT&T, replace Western Union at the pinnacle of corporate power, and become synonymous with one of the great technological milestones in history. And all of these changes were wrought by a trio of underfinanced entrepreneurs.

Another Technological Crossroad

One hundred twenty-one years have passed since Orton's great miscalculation, and communications is at another crossroad. Technological achievements—especially the digitization of information and its transmission over the Internet—are changing the world anew, just as the telephone once did. These advances have been compounded by equally powerful changes in public policy. Governments around the world are eliminating hundred-year-old monopoly regulations. Taken together, these lightning bolts have created the greatest turmoil in communications since Bell unleashed the telephone upon the world. And once again, entrepreneurs are playing a decisive role in the new market, just as the Bell Telephone Co. did in the late 19th century.

"We still move the vast majority of information over a network that was designed at the turn of the century," says Jim Crowe, the ground-breaking entrepreneur who helped launch Metropolitan Fiber Systems (MFS), the local phone company acquired by WorldCom in 1996. "We have automated the process, but the fundamental technology is exactly what it was. We are now at the end of the life-cycle of that technology."

The rise of the Internet and other new technologies is creating a historic opportunity for entrepreneurs to construct new high-speed data networks, develop new multimedia services, and help the world through the transition. A generation of powerful new companies is in formation. MFS is an indication of what's to come. The company had a market capitalization of $800 million when it issued its first stock to the public in May 1993. WorldCom paid $14.3 billion for MFS in 1996. And a $100 investment in WorldCom in 1989 was worth more than $3,137 in September 1997. A comparable investment in AT&T was worth $198.

Crowe compares the shakeup in telecommunications to Bell Telephone's ascension over Western Union, or Microsoft and Intel's ascension over IBM in the computer business. The telecommunications network is shaping the world today as the personal computer drove change during the previous 15 years. "The mid-eighties and early nineties were the PC era. We're in the network era today. That is certainly where the value is being created," Crowe says. He is right back where he started, building new high-capacity, data-oriented telecommunications networks with construction company Peter Kiewit & Sons, reflecting his conviction that the opportunities for entrepreneurs in telecommunications are wide open.

"When you have major changes in technology at work,

the folks who dominated the old era rarely come to dominate the new era," says Crowe, who is now running Kiewit Diversified, a Kiewit spin-off building networks optimized for the Internet and capable of being upgraded at will.

"It's like AT&T versus Western Union all over again," says entrepreneur David McCourt, the chairman and chief executive of RCN (Residential Communications Network) Corp., which is building high-capacity local networks for residential customers, just as MFS built them for businesses. "And it's going to make more people rich than the industrial revolution did. More money will be made by entrepreneurs in this industry than by anything else in this country's history."

New Companies Will Lead the Way

McCourt, a veteran of MFS and a former board member of WorldCom, says the telecommunications market is entering a period of enormous growth and that entrepreneurs are ideally positioned to lead it. The U.S. market for local and long-distance phone service will rise 37 percent to $255 billion in 2001, up from $186 billion in 1997, International Data Corp. (IDC) says. Competitive local exchange carriers, which held 1.4 percent of the local market in 1997, will generate the most growth, the research group reports. IDC expects these entrepreneurial companies, which are building networks that compete with the Bells and GTE, to capture 8.4 percent of the market by 2001. The Bells' share of the market will drop 6 percentage points to 32 percent, and the long-distance carriers' share will hold steady at about 46 percent of the market, IDC says.

New companies will generate the real growth while the giants of yesterday steal each other's market share and consume themselves with mergers and acquisitions, McCourt says. He predicts that the U.S. telecommunications market, including the cable TV market, which generated about $27 billion in 1997 subscriber revenues, will reach $350 billion in five to seven years. New technology will create new services and make older industries such as video stores obsolete, McCourt says. And that growth projection doesn't include the $23 billion wireless phone market, which is growing 30 percent a year, or the Internet.

"The opportunity belongs to the entrepreneur. It's been like that for 100 years," McCourt says. The great start-ups are always born in someone's garage or basement. They aren't born inside a large company. Microsoft wasn't born in the bowels of IBM; it was born in a garage. And MFS wasn't born within a giant phone company; it was created in the office of a construction company in Omaha.

Top executives are already leaving the country's big established phone companies to start new ventures of their own. AT&T wireless chief Jim Barkesdale launched Netscape. AT&T president Alex Mandl started wireless venture Teligent, and AT&T consumer unit chief Joe Nacchio is CEO of Qwest, which is building a new coast-to-coast fiber-optic network. They recognize that the biggest opportunities in the new market belong to the entrepreneur. The exceptions to this rule will be the big companies that adopt an entrepreneurial culture that values action and risk.

Large companies simply can't move as fast as small entrepreneurs. Bound by bureaucracy and regulation, they are unable to move as quickly. And with huge markets to protect, they can't afford to take the risks that come naturally to smaller companies. Case in point: The Telecommunications Act of 1996 required the regional Bell phone companies to open their local markets to competition, and the Bells have failed to roam beyond their borders and invade each other's territory. They have been merging with each other instead. And the big long-distance companies have moved into the local market on a very limited basis.

Meanwhile, McCourt has started a new company to take advantage of the new law. RCN is building in the residential market what MFS built in the business market: a state-of-the-art fiber-optic network to compete with the Bells.

The fiber runs all the way to the customer's building, allowing RCN to deliver advanced services to its customers' doorsteps. He has already begun operations in Boston and New York, in the heart of Bell Atlantic-Nynex territory, where he's offering local and long-distance phone service, high-speed Internet access, and cable television with interactive features derived from the Internet.

Finding Micro-niches

Instead of trying to cater to the mass market, as phone companies traditionally do, RCN is targeting its services at carefully defined niches. After RCN identified the cities and neighborhoods where it wanted to operate, it took a giant step further and targeted specific buildings in New York and Boston. In its Manhattan office, located just a few blocks north of the former Nynex headquarters on the Avenue of the Americas, a map is covered with dots that represent hundreds of large apartment houses with affluent, high-spending customers. That sort of focus is just one example of how the old mass telecommunications market is dying. In its place, a mass of interconnected niche markets is growing, defined by geography, demographics, and the boundless variety of customers and needs. Each one represents another opportunity for the entrepreneur.

Meanwhile, Bell Atlantic spent the last two years buying Nynex, expending enormous amounts of energy overcoming regulatory obstacles to the deal. Bell Atlantic plans metropolitan networks comparable to RCN's, but the first one isn't scheduled to begin operations until at least 1999 in Philadelphia. New York and Boston will have to wait, giving RCN an opportunity to strike first.

MCI's entry into the local market has been running steep losses, which derailed the sale of the company to British Telecommunications. AT&T has ventured into the local market even more slowly.

Yet the entrepreneurs aren't waiting for the market to develop for proof that the venture will work. "There is no market to speak of. You have to believe it is going to come," entrepreneur David Friend says. He developed the ARP synthesizer in the 1970s and was an early entrant in the personal computer revolution of the 1980s. His next move: a telecommunications network that specializes in the transmission of faxes.

FaxNet reflects a new type of telecommunications carrier: a carefully targeted niche service that penetrates a market the big players haven't the time or interest to explore. These smaller companies are taking advantage of the convergence of the telecommunications network and the computer, writing special software programs for the telephone instead of the PC.

No one expects the current giants of the telecommunications industry to disappear or become irrelevant. But there is plenty of room for newcomers who can envision where the world is going next and have conviction and the competence to act on that vision, even at great personal risk. These are the hallmarks of the entrepreneur. They are crucial assets in any business, especially one that is changing as quickly and relentlessly as telecommunications. It's been that way for more than a hundred years. Western Union had the opportunity and the money to buy Bell Telephone's patents. It let the chance slip by because it didn't understand where the world was headed. By the time the demand for this new technology was apparent — by the time stock brokers were clamoring for it — the battle was over and Western Union had been toppled by a tiny start-up that became AT&T.

The Forces of Change

The entrepreneurial nature of New England Telephone quickly evolved into something much different as the company moved from Boston to New York and became AT&T in 1899. That shift extinguished the entrepreneurial character of the telephone industry, too, for the better part of a century.

Bell himself retired from the business in 1878 and dedicated the rest of his life to scientific research. He went on to invent the stethoscope and devices to aid in the instruction of the deaf. The company brought in Theodore Vail, a 33-year-old post office manager, as general manager that same year. He immediately began to consolidate the company's power. New England Telephone acquired smaller phone companies and, before long, it owned more than 90 percent of the country's telephone lines. It changed its name to American Telephone & Telegraph Corp. in 1899, a name that reflected its new national character. It also moved its offices to the country's financial capital in lower Manhattan.

The company's power drew skepticism from antitrust regulators in Washington, who feared its market power from

Theodore N. Vail, 1878.

Property of AT&T Archives. Reprinted with permission of AT&T.

the very beginning. The local phone business wasn't a monopoly in the early years. Half of the phone markets in the country were served by more than one company in 1902. But AT&T gained a powerful edge in 1913 by acquiring the rights to the audion, a signal booster that made good-quality long-distance service possible for the first time. AT&T refused to connect competing local phone companies to its long-distance network, thereby pressuring the competition to sell out to the growing behemoth.

AT&T had already drawn unwelcome attention from the antitrust regulators at the Justice Department during the previous year. The company proposed a settlement with the government in 1913. The agreement, named for AT&T

vice president Nathan Kingsbury, forced AT&T to halt its string of acquisitions, connect its competitors to its long-distance network, and sell Western Union, which it had acquired a few years before. The company's role as a monopoly was institutionalized in the Communications Act of 1934, which allowed AT&T to dominate the market in exchange for providing cheap local service to the masses.

AT&T's Marvel of Technology

The network that developed under this system was a marvel of technology—unquestionably the greatest communications system the world had yet seen. By the 1950s it reached more than 70 percent of the population of the United States, the highest penetration in the world. The quality was unmatched. Nearly every call was completed, and quickly. Static and interference from other calls were minimal. The company's research arm, Bell Laboratories, lived up to the standards of its namesake. The lab was a premier source for basic research, and its inventions included the cellular phone in the 1940s, followed by the first transatlantic telephone cable, the first transistor, and the first communications satellite.

Yet, for all its grandeur, the government was never quite comfortable with the enormous company and its power. AT&T exercised absolute control over the system. The government chipped away at AT&T's power during the latter half of the 20th century, gradually building up to the huge changes now underway. The Justice Department toyed with the idea of breaking up AT&T altogether in the 1950s, and even filed an antitrust suit. But the settlement, known as a *final judgment*, stopped well short of that. AT&T agreed to sell its patent on the cellular phone, and it agreed to stay out of the computer market, which was in the early stages of development.

Entrepreneurs would soon win greater concessions. Regulators allowed major phone users to set up private microwave communications systems in 1959. A company called

Microwave Communications Inc. (MCI) made a landmark request in 1963: It wanted to use the radio spectrum to provide a public alternative to AT&T's long-distance service. The request was finally approved in 1969, opening the way for the return of the entrepreneur to telecommunications. MCI began offering service in 1972. MCI was offering its Execunet long-distance service by 1974, allowing anyone with a phone to tap into the MCI network by dialing a special code before each long-distance call.

The Justice Department filed an antitrust suit two years later that eventually led to the spinoff of AT&T's century-old local phone service in 1984. The Bell System was divided into seven separate companies known as the *regional Bells*—Nynex, Bell Atlantic, and BellSouth in the East; Ameritech in the Midwest; and Southwestern Bell, US West, and Pacific Telesis in the West. AT&T kept long-distance, Bell labs, and the equipment-manufacturing division.

All hell was about to break loose in the long-distance market, though.

AT&T was forced to sell its service to competitors at wholesale prices, allowing them to resell it to the public. That dramatically increased the number of competitors in the market. The government also eliminated the cumbersome dialing codes that customers had to use with each call to bypass AT&T's network and use a competitor's. Finally, in the early 1990s, the government forced AT&T to lower its wholesale rates, intensifying the flood of competitors into the long-distance market.

By the mid-1990s, long-distance was ruled by an oligopoly of AT&T, MCI, and Sprint, controlling about 90 percent of the market. The rest was shared by hundreds of resellers and a small, elite band of companies that were building independent networks. It's debatable how much good this did for the consumer. Prices began to fall, although many observers say they didn't fall nearly as much as they should have. Professor Michael Noll, of the University of Southern California, says long-distance prices have been steadily falling about 4 percent a year throughout the century (in constant, inflation-adjusted dollars), and that the pace didn't increase with the breakup of AT&T.

There's no question that entrepreneurs made out well, though. A new generation of companies appeared in four or five years. They relied on discount-pricing and direct-sales techniques and moved swiftly into the tiny market niches that the big players overlooked. Some of them—such as WorldCom, LCI, Excel, and its merger partner, Vartec—are now multi-billion-dollar companies.

All of the incremental changes in the market have cleared the way for the next developments, which will be far more dramatic. Many of the basic characteristics of the telecommunications market have persisted through the late 19th century right up to now.

⊡ Most importantly—and most fundamentally—it has been defined around the transmission of the human voice.

⊡ The technology of the phone and the network is a direct descendant of Alexander Graham Bell's original designs.

⊡ Phones have been pretty much stationary things, tethered to the network with a cord.

⊡ Monopolies have prevailed. The local market in the United States has been mostly ruled by monopolies that date from the late 19th century, competition in the long-distance market notwithstanding. And there's been next to no competition in the global market, where service has been reserved for nationally based monopolies run by governments, or tied closely to them.

Telecommunications Redefined

All of these assumptions are being challenged. The network is no longer defined around the human voice. The word "telephone" was coined by Bell from two Greek words, *tele* meaning distant, and *phone* meaning sound. It was a perfect description in its day, but now the network is carrying all sorts of information from video to other types of digitized data. In a few years, computer data will actually exceed voice traffic on the network, and the multimedia boom will follow. The more general word "telecommunications" is a better description today. The wireless phone is an increasingly common supplement to the traditional corded phone. And national monopolies are being replaced by competitive global markets.

These changes have been powered by the twin engines of technology and public policy, which kicked in simultaneously and created the most quickly changing market in the world.

The technological change is, in a word, the Internet.

It began in the late 1960s as a way for Defense Department researchers and academics to communicate with each other by computer. It was known as ARPANET in those days, for the Advanced Research Projects Network. It evolved into a communications system for hardcore computer types even as other forms of online communications blossomed in the 1980s and early 1990s. Consumers paid to use much simpler, private online networks, such as Prodigy, CompuServe, and America Online (AOL). That all changed when Netscape Communications introduced a software program that allowed consumers to "navigate" the Internet as easily as they dialed into AOL. And the best part was, the Internet itself was free. The only charge was for the physical connection. It was like paying for a train ticket to a theme park and getting all the rides for free.

One of those "rides" was awfully similar to the telephone. Computer enthusiasts with the right software could suddenly place international phone calls for the price of their local connection to the Internet. The rest of the call was free. Their voices were converted to the ones and zeroes of computer language, and travelled across the Internet just like any other form of data. The Internet couldn't tell the difference between a voice transmission and an e-mail message. Data was data. Sure, "phone calls" over "the Net" were slow, the quality was poor, and people had to take turns talking as they would over a walkie-talkie. Even worse, they needed a computer with special software at each end of the call. But it was free.

The phone network operates pretty much as it did in Bell's day. Millions of simple receivers and transmitters, known as telephones, convert the human voice into electrical impulses, which are carried across a network of thin copper wires, microwave towers, and fiber-optic cables. Each phone call travels along its own circuit, the equivalent of having its own lane on an incredibly wide highway. That allows each call to move quickly and without interference from other traffic.

The Internet is based on an entirely different technology. Voice is converted into computer data, and broken into "packets" of information. The fundamental difference in the network is that conversations or communications between one computer and another don't have their own separate circuit. Millions of computers share circuits. Each packet travels along the first circuit that is available. They are all supposed to end up in the right place because all the packets from a particular transmission — phone call, e-mail message, or video clip—share an identifying code so they won't get lost.

Of course, sometimes the packets don't always arrive in the right order, or sometimes they arrive a little late. Hence, the difficulty of using this technology for a live communication, such as a phone call. It's much better suited to sending other kinds of data.

Yet, for all its trouble, "packet" switching is more efficient than the traditional phone network. When people talk over the Internet, they only tie up a circuit for the time it takes to send a packet of information. On the traditional phone network, a circuit is tied up as long as the parties are connected, including the pauses between words and sentences, or the time it takes to answer the door bell. A packet-switched network would simply reassign the circuit to another user. That's one reason it's so cheap to send a call over the Internet.

If the inconvenience of phone calls over the Internet can be overcome (and it will), then telephone companies face their biggest challenge yet. It won't be another case of one company undercutting another company's price, as MCI did in its battle with AT&T. It will be the sort of challenge that the telephone presented to the telegraph. Telephone companies could lose $8 billion in global revenue as voice and fax calls migrate to the Internet by 2001, according to Action Information Services, a consulting company in Falls Church, Virginia.

The Internet's Impact

A few companies, such as USA Global Link, are already making money by using the Internet to circumvent particularly expensive phone networks in other countries. Some of those countries are outlawing such activity, because it threatens the profits of state-run phone monopolies. But the big phone companies in developed countries see that the world is changing. AT&T expects to lose 16 percent of its phone traffic to the Internet within five years. MCI is building a packet-switched network so that it's ready to make the switch when the time comes. It even hired Internet pioneer Vint Cerf to lead its Internet unit.

The Internet threatens to change the nature of telecommunications itself. But it's also driving the greatest change and the greatest growth in telecommunications. Consumers and business are buying additional phone lines for their computers. And the time they spend on-line increases revenue for *local* phone networks, which act as toll bridges between computers and the Internet.

The Internet is just one of several powerful technologies that are changing telecommunications. Among the others:

THE FORCES OF CHANGE   35

The computer itself

The computer makes it possible to create all sorts of new features, such as Caller ID and Call Waiting. Phone companies are becoming more like computer software companies, writing software for high-tech digital phones and networks instead of PCs. New businesses and industries are being created around those features. One example will send a hotel-style wake-up call to your phone. Another example is David Friend's FaxNet. He has written software that makes sure fax lines on his phone network are never busy. Coming next: services that combine corded and cordless phones, pagers, fax machines, and computer on a single number; services that will convert written e-mail messages and faxes into an electronic voice and read them over the phone, or convert voice-mail messages into e-mail messages. Other features will help users figure out the cheapest long-distance service. They are transforming the phone from a simple transmitter and receiver into an appliance that helps people manage communications of many varieties.

The wireless phone

This technological milestone was invented by AT&T in the 1940s, but the first commercial networks didn't begin operation in the United States until the 1980s. Now the industry is worth $23 billion and growing at a rate of 30 percent a year. The wireless phone could eventually displace the traditional corded phone. But it's also a source of growth for traditional phone companies, since calls placed from wireless phones intersect with their wired networks.

These new technologies have fueled incredible growth in telecommunications. Households that had a single phone number a generation ago often have additional lines now for a fax machine, a wireless phone, a computer, and a pager. And people are spending more time using the network. The average voice call lasts three to five minutes, but people often spend hours on the Internet, maintaining a local phone

Telecom Growth

	1997	2000	%
Local Exchange	$53.6	$62.0	16
Long Distance	$86.6	$104.0	20
Cable TV (subscription)	$27.7	$29.8	8
Cable TV (advertising)	$4.2	$4.9	17
Wireless Service revenues	$24.9	$48.2	94
Global Telecommunications	$725.0	$950.0	31
Internet revenues (business access)	$2.0	$7.1	255
Internet revenues (consumer access)	$4.2	$7.6	81
Internet, business to business (transactions)	$7.0	$134.0	1814
Internet, business to consumer (transactions)	$2.7	$10.0	270

Source: The Yankee Group (revenue in billions)

connection all the while.

All of these technological changes have been compounded by equally big changes in public policy around the world. The Telecommunications Act of 1996 triggered the elimination of local monopolies in the United States. The following year, countries around the world agreed to dismantle their telecommunications monopolies under the General Agreement on Tariffs and Trade. The European Union is scheduled to open its markets in 1998. Huge markets are available to competition—to entrepreneurs—for the first time ever.

And those markets are growing. Half the people in the world have never even used a phone, but that is changing. Latin America, Africa, Asia, and Eastern Europe are developing fast. There are only 200 phone lines per 1,000 people in the developing markets of the Pacific, and there are only 100 lines for 1,000 people in developing markets elsewhere around the world, says David Roddy, telecommunications economist at Deloitte & Touche Consulting Group. There are 700 lines per 1,000 people in the United States.

The rest of the world is going to catch up. That demand creates enormous opportunities for entrepreneurs, and liberal new trade policies allow them to pursue it. Telecommunications networks are at the core of a new global economy that is based on information. People must transmit, analyze, and manage huge amounts of information on a global basis, 24 hours a day, seven days a week. The old computer networks of the 1980s—small, private, and expensive groups of PCs—won't cut it anymore. People need large, inexpensive systems that are at once open and secure, that integrate all of their information, and that make information easier to manage. They need systems that can handle massive amounts of information. In short, they need telecommunications.

It's no accident that the monopoly rules that dominated telecommunications for a century are crumbling now. The market is too complex, the demand too great, for any one company, or group of companies, to satisfy them all. There is an urgent need for more robust networks, for more specialized services, and for lower prices. That sort of innovation isn't possible in a monopoly environment. The market has demanded more competition, which has created opportunity for the entrepreneur at every level—from the capital-intensive construction of global networks to small, specialized niche services.

Economics and Opportunities

Scale: Is Bigger Better?

Experts have long argued that the economics of the telecommunications market are overwhelmingly in favor of big companies. That belief has been the driving force in the mergers and acquisitions that have swept through the industry during the last few years: SBC Communications and Pacific Telesis, Bell Atlantic and Nynex, WorldCom and its pending union with MCI. Bigger companies have greater purchasing power, and they have the ability to begin and end more calls over their own network, without sharing revenue with another company that must carry the call somewhere along the way. Most important, they have bigger bases of customers, which can be used as a foundation to sell more products.

The value of a network increases exponentially as more people use it. "The value of a network is the square of the number of places it connects," MFS founder Jim Crowe says. "If you have a network that connects to ten places it is

worth a lot more than twice as much as a network that connects to five."

It also takes a lot of money to get most communications
ventures started. The capital costs of building a network
are enormous. Even companies that don't build their own
networks face big costs tied to marketing and regulation. It
costs about three times as much to acquire a new customer
as it does to retain an existing account, according to Ophelia
Barsketis, senior vice president at Stein Roe & Farnham,
an investment firm in Chicago.

"It's an awful hard industry in which to be a small company, as far as I can see," says David Roddy, chief telecommunications analyst at Deloitte & Touche Consulting
Group. "There are some niche markets the small player
can develop. But once it becomes profitable, the big guys
will take over."

This argument is true, but it only describes a part of the
market. Massive scale is important to a certain kind of telecommunications company, the sort of big, familiar entity
that delivers basic service to lots of people. Most of the giants that dominate the market today will survive in one form
or another, and many of them will prosper. But even if an
oligopoly of three to five companies rules 90 percent of the
new telecommunications market, as an oligopoly ruled long-
distance, that still leaves a $20 billion to $30 billion market
for the entrepreneur, not counting the new opportunities
created by the Internet.

"I think one of the big fallacies here is that big is better,"
says Jack Grubman, head of global telecommunications research at Salomon Smith Barney. "The major companies
feel scale and scope is imperative. If they made the *a priori*
decision that they are going to be global players, they probably have to be gigantic. But at the end of the day, the guys
actually doing the integrated bundling are these smaller
guys, who are targeted around either customer niches or
geographic niches."

Scale was more important in the days when phone

companies sold one or two basic services. The only way to grow under those circumstances was to add more customers. Changes in regulation and technology now allow companies to grow by selling more services without necessarily adding more customers. Some big companies, such as AT&T and MCI, are actually scaling back—reducing their customer bases to focus on the more lucrative segments of the market.

And many big, established local phone companies are trying to reinvent themselves as their opposites—competitive local exchange carriers. GTE and BellSouth, for example, are separating their services company and their network. The traditional regulated company maintains control of the physical network and satisfies the company's legal requirement to provide basic local phone service to the masses. Meanwhile, these companies are setting up smaller, unregulated entities that buy access to the network, just like any entrepreneur, and resell it to small, highly-targeted markets.

Bryan Van Dussen, of The Yankee Group, believes the entire telecommunications market will be restructured in this manner, creating a small group of enormous companies that own and operate infrastructure, and a large number of companies that sell service to sharply defined segments of the market.

Entrepreneurs are often well-suited to exploiting these incremental opportunities, where quick decision-making, low overhead, and proximity to the customer are crucial. Newer companies aren't burdened with "legacy" systems, an industry term for obsolete or outmoded equipment. They generally don't have to negotiate expensive and rule-bound contracts with huge union work forces. And new local phone companies aren't legally required to provide service to everyone in their territory, as the regional Bells are. No longer bound by the social goal of universal service, they are free to seek the most attractive customers, just as RCN is doing in New York, Washington, and Boston. Entrepreneurs also typically employ the latest technology, benefiting from the falling price and rising power of computers and network infrastructure. That gives them a natural advantage in the race to make the best, most efficient use of capital.

It's the rationale behind Philip Anschutz's Qwest, which is laying high-tech fiber-optic lines across the country. Qwest CEO Joe Nacchio, a former AT&T executive, says Qwest's 13,000-route-mile network was cheaper to build than older, competing networks, and that it can pass its savings along to customers.

"Qwest will have the lowest-cost, highest-technology network available, and will have abundant capacity to supply resellers in very large volumes," Merrill Lynch said in a July 1997 report. Qwest is a big, well-capitalized company, but compared to the AT&Ts and BTs of the world, it's a relatively small start-up.

"Scale is important to those who own infrastructure and have a mass-market mentality," says Van Dussen, of The Yankee Group. "If you don't own infrastructure and you aren't concerned about the mass market, I'm not so sure scale is important." More important to their success, Van Dussen says, is a first-rate, easy-to-use information system that allows for the quick development of custom products.

This is not to say that scale is irrelevant to the success of a new venture. It only means that huge scale isn't necessary to be successful. Young telecommunications companies must grow as quickly as possible to achieve critical mass. Many such ventures require substantial investments in capital equipment, regulatory approval, and marketing. Losses are inevitable in the early stages of any telecommunications business. Every entrepreneur in this field must be prepared for losses during the early stages. But those who have the resources and the management skill to achieve critical mass find that the economics turn sharply in their favor, says Barsketis of Stein Roe & Farnham. That's because many of the big capital costs are fixed, while growth is not. As the business grows, costs decrease as a percentage of revenue.

"If you have a pipe in the ground, it costs as much to have 1,000 customers as it does to have 100 customers, once you have made the initial investments," she says. "If you just increase (the traffic) a little bit, it's amazing how profitable it can be."

Rising Competition, Rising Demand

Phone profits were inflated for many years by government-protected monopolies. Carriers operated without threat of competition, and state regulators guaranteed them a profit. No reasonable business could fail under such circumstances. It would be a huge mistake, however, to assume that they couldn't have prospered without government help. The underlying economics of the communications business were strong, and they remain so today. True, the economics of the new competitive market are different in many respects from the old monopoly environment, and in some ways they are worse. Competition changes everything. Profit margins are narrowing, and the risks and uncertainty are severe. Yet demand is strong, the market is growing, and companies are operating more efficiently than ever before. On top of that, operating a communications business is simply a good investment for those who can achieve critical mass.

"I think every aspect of the communications business is attractive. I think there is something in every sector," Barsketis says. The industry is still extremely profitable. Rising competition, lawsuits, controversy over regulations, mergers, huge capital investments, management turmoil, and volatile stock prices often obscure the fact that this is still a very profitable business. The price of telecommunications services still far exceeds the cost of providing it. Cash-flow margins in telecommunications far exceed average margins for the Standard & Poor's 500, says Jack Grubman, head of global telecommunications research at Salomon Smith Barney in New York. He expects them to worsen, however, in the next few years, especially for the big, established carriers. But for now they are strong:

· ·

⊡ Cash-flow margins for the regional Bell companies, the giants of the local sector, are 40 to 45 percent, compared with 20 to 25 percent for the S&P 500.

⊡ Margins in the more competitive long-distance sector aren't as good, but they still beat the overall stock market at 30 percent.

"The economic conditions today are very strong. However, I would argue that will come under pressure," Grubman says. "The economics of this business over the next five years will get worse, not better, especially for the incumbents. Growth could be the entrepreneurs' if they execute on their strategy and raise the capital necessary to build their networks."

The economics of the business are most often described in terms of rising competition, and for good reason. Every new opportunity created by public policy or technology creates a corresponding increase in competition. There are at least 800 contenders in the long-distance market, where AT&T once had a monopoly just a generation ago. There could soon be as many as eight licensed wireless carriers in some cities that had only two a few years ago. Competition is gaining momentum in the local market, too, even if most people believe it should be developing faster. All of these markets are converging into a new telecommunications sector. And the Internet is hanging over the whole thing, adding another dimension to the competition.

There is another great economic force in telecommunications, though: the unprecedented demand for all kinds of communications. "It's like GM suddenly discovered that everyone wants three cars, not one-point-one," says Bell Atlantic Chairman and CEO Ray Smith. He believes demand will easily outpace the growth in competition during the next three to five years, comparing it to the high-growth PC market of the last ten years. Bell Atlantic's wireless business is increasing its number of customers at a pace of 20 to 30 percent a year. Revenue from any sort of enhanced service, such as Caller ID or three-way calling, is growing at a rate of 30 percent a year. The number of high-speed ISDN phone lines is growing 40 percent a year, thanks to insatiable demand for quick connections to the Internet. New businesses are being created by the new emphasis on data transmission. Bell Atlantic, for example, has a new unit known as Network Integration, which helps customers combine and manage their various types of communications. It's growing 35 percent a year. The growth at Bell Atlantic reflects the demand that is sweeping through the entire market.

These broad forces of supply and demand vary throughout the local, long-distance, and wireless sectors. The Internet and multimedia markets add additional layers of complexity. These sectors are rapidly converging, and few companies define themselves with a single service anymore. Yet they retain distinct characteristics and dynamics after decades of separation.

Long-Distance Opportunities

The $75 billion long-distance market provided the first great telecommunications opportunity for U.S. entrepreneurs since deregulation began in the 1960s with the appearance of MCI. It created two new industry giants, MCI and Sprint. And the second and third waves of long-distance competitors, such as LCI and Excel, have evolved from small resellers into multi-billion-dollar companies with their own fiber-optic networks. Incredibly, there is still money to be made in traditional voice long-distance, at least for the next few years.

Yes, competition is rising, and the economics are deteriorating, but it's mostly a problem for AT&T, MCI, and other big carriers. Their marketing costs are skyrocketing as entrepreneurs undermine them. Life is better right now for the entrepreneurs themselves. That's because the wholesale price of a long-distance call is falling, but the retail price is relatively stable. Merrill Lynch estimates that the

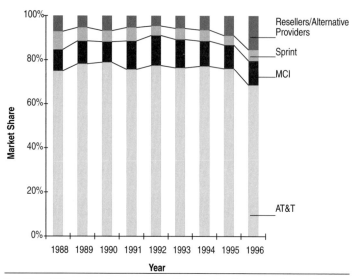

Resellers/Alternative Carriers Gain Share in the Consumer Long-Distance Market (1988–1996)

Source: The Yankee Group TAP Survey, 1987–1996

average wholesale rate dropped to 1.5 to 2 cents a minute, excluding access charges, in mid-1997, down from 4.5 cents a minute in 1992. The retail price, excluding access charges, was 10 cents in 1996, little changed from 11 cents in 1992.

"This wider spread (8.5 cents in 1996 vs. 6.5 cents a minute in 1992) allows for much more attractive profits and/or aggressive pricing by resellers trying to take market share," Merrill Lynch reports. Meanwhile, the Big Three started to feel the pressure from general resellers, dial-around companies, and prepaid calling card services in 1996, forcing them to cut prices and raise marketing expenditures, Merrill Lynch says. This opportunity doesn't last forever, though. The average retail price of a long-distance call will fall during the next three years, possibly to as low as 6 cents a minute, Merrill Lynch forecasts. The pace of the decrease depends upon how quickly the Bells enter the long-distance market.

Other big opportunities in domestic long-distance

revolve around data transmission. There's a huge demand for high-speed data connections, and that demand will increase as video phone calls and other multimedia services become more important to businesses and consumers. AT&T says its data-transmission business is growing 30 to 40 percent a year. There isn't enough capacity on the existing network to meet that demand. There's a lot of money to be made building new lines and networks.

"There is a real scarcity of fiber capacity out there, especially long-haul fiber," Grubman says. In fact, his firm, Salomon Smith Barney, helped bring Qwest public in an effort to tap that demand. Needless to say, this is an extremely capital-intensive business. AT&T spent about $7 billion in 1997 alone upgrading its long-distance network.

Building Local Networks

This entire $100 billion market is in the throes of change. Its century-old monopoly rules have been eliminated, and companies are preparing to do battle. Competition is steadily increasing in the residential sector, even though it's developing more slowly than some people expected. Competition for business accounts has been growing for years, and it has already produced a generation of entrepreneurs such as Brooks Fiber, Teleport and MFS, which is now part of WorldCom.

The residential side of the business is the last monopoly, or near monopoly, in U.S. telecommunications. Strategies for competing in this crucial market generate the hottest debates in the industry, and billions of dollars are at stake. There are three paths into the local market, and each one is strewn with obstacles. The most profitable path is to build and operate your own network, but that costs a fortune. "The Telecommunications Act assumed that competition would develop in the local market the way it did in long-distance, but they are completely different," says Scott Cleland, director of Legg Mason's Precursor Group. Local area networks are much more expensive.

⊡ There are 6.2 million kilometers of local network wires in the United States vs. 150,000 kilometers of long-distance wire.

⊡ The combined value of those local networks is about $270 billion vs. a combined value of $40 billion in long-distance assets.

"The local phone business is an extremely capital-intensive, highly regulated, complex business. It's very hard to replicate on a broad scale," Cleland says. "People can go in and replicate a small portion, but to replicate it on a wide scale is enormously difficult. It means digging up streets and serving the local customer. That is manpower-intensive and cost-intensive."

Few companies are willing to spend billions of dollars in a market where the rules are still being written and customer demand is subject to debate. AT&T, with all its money and power, is waiting to see how demand develops before it sinks billions into the business. MCI is constructing local networks in about 60 markets. But its losses were $400 million in 1997 alone, about twice as high as it expected. Losses for 1998 will be the same or higher. Few companies have the money to survive those initial investments. A handful of companies, such as Teleport and Brooks Fiber, have built their own networks in the business market. Few companies can match their access to capital.

Local networks are difficult to build, but they can be extremely profitable once a company achieves critical mass. A local network has enormous strategic value as well. It allows the provider to establish a direct connection with the customer, and that can be used as a foundation for selling additional services. A significant number of people will also demand the convenience of buying most or all of their communications from a single company. By combining local, long-distance, Internet access, and cable television on a single wire, RCN's David McCourt says he can reduce his selling, general, and administrative costs to a level below that of competing phone and cable companies that offer fewer services.

Companies that want to enter the local market have several alternatives to network infrastructure construction. The up-front costs are much lower, but the profit margins are slimmer, too. Those alternatives are known as *total service* resale and *unbundled* resale. Total service resale allows an entrepreneur to buy access to a local phone company's entire network—including switches and transmission lines—at a discount. Then it resells the service to the public using its own name. Unbundled resellers, on the other hand, have some of their own equipment, a switch perhaps. They take just what they need from the local phone company, which is cheaper than buying the entire "bundle."

Many analysts readily dismiss these two options. "Local doesn't lend itself to resale," Grubman says. Few resellers have been able to negotiate a big enough discount from the local phone company to cover their costs and still make a profit. Average wholesale discounts are about 20 percent. Local rates, especially for residential service, are low to begin with, leaving little room for resellers. It's different than the long-distance market, which spawned waves of profitable resellers. Long-distance rates were extremely high. Big long-distance companies could afford to give resellers relatively generous discounts—up to 70 percent off the retail price.

Resellers often complain of other problems as well. The company that sells them wholesale service is also their competitor in the retail market, raising a potential conflict of interest. Resellers must rely on this competitor to give them quick, easy access to their customers.

There are a few people willing to make the case for the local resale business, though. One of them is Richard Notebart, the chairman and chief executive officer of Ameritech, the big local phone company in the Midwest. "You don't need lots of capital. You need a billing system and salespeople… If you can stay lean and have discipline, it's a great business," he says. The viability of the resale business varies from one market to the next, because local phone companies have different attitudes toward entrepreneurs and resellers. Ameritech says it is trying to court them with relatively deep discounts—closer to 25 percent than 20 percent. US Networks, one of the first local resellers in the country, got its start in Ameritech territory in Ohio.

The Growing Wireless Market

Wireless is one of the great growth markets in the world. The number of new subscribers increased from 29 million in 1995 to about 53 million in 1996, Merrill Lynch says. Much of that growth is occurring in Europe and the Asia/Pacific region. The U.S. Cellular Trade Industry Association says that subscriber growth in the United States was 37 percent in the United States between 1988 and 1996. However, the size of the average local cellular bill in the United States fell from $97 a month to $48 a month. "New subscribers were more reluctant to make cellular calls than were early users," Merrill said, citing relatively high airtime charges in years past. The average capital cost per customer is $907, meaning it can take several years for a company to recoup its investment.

Competition is rising in the U.S. market. The federal government limited competition to two companies in each market until just a few years ago. There could soon be eight new competitors in each market, although few markets will see battle on that scale. The cost of buying a license, building a network, and marketing to customers is high. The stock and bond markets have soured on these companies, making it difficult for them to raise capital. They are having trouble making installment payments on the licenses they bought in Federal Communications Commission (FCC) auctions. One company has sought bankruptcy protection, and others may follow.

Most wireless carriers have their own networks, but the resale market is growing. MCI, a pioneer in this area, is buying service from NextWave Communications, offering a preview of how smaller companies will resell service.

The International Market

Conditions in the international market are among the strongest in the world. Economic development is surging across vast swaths of the globe, from East Asia to Latin America, and those regions need more phones. Demand for additional lines is enormous. People wait for a year or more to receive a phone in Brazil. The opportunity in these markets is akin to the opportunity AT&T found in the United States in the 19th century. These markets have been controlled by government-sanctioned monopolies that have charged exorbitant rates. Now governments are opening these markets to competition, creating huge opportunities for global companies to build new wireless and landline networks, offering customers in these regions better service at lower rates.

It's a slam-dunk right now to undercut the ridiculous prices of government-run monopolies. But the game will get tougher in the next five years as these monopolies lower their prices. The arbitrage game will be over within five years. The opportunities will be enormous, but the markets will be closer in feel to other developed markets. Prices are falling, and demand is surging. Entering these markets also requires a lot of capital and experience in doing business abroad. The competition is also fierce: Global alliances such as BT-MCI, Sprint-Deutsche Telekom and France Telecom, AT&T-Unisource, and the rapidly expanding operations of BellSouth, SBC, and Bell Atlantic, are moving quickly.

The Huge Equipment Market

AT&T spun off its Lucent Technologies equipment-making division and its Bell Laboratories research house at the end of 1996. It turned out to be the biggest public offering in U.S. history, raising $3.3 billion. The shares, issued at $26, have tripled in value since then, reflecting the amazing strength of the telecommunications equipment market. Services companies such as AT&T, MCI, and the Bells are locked in a grinding war of attrition, and all the combatants need equipment. It matters little to Lucent who wins the war in the services sector, as long as the orders keep flowing.

The global market for telecommunications equipment was $160 billion in 1996, Merrill Lynch analyst Michael Ching says. The $30 billion market for switches—the computers that connect one phone line to another to complete a call—is growing 10 percent a year. The $8 billion access market is growing 30 percent a year, and the $25 billion transmission market is growing about 6 percent, although some niches are growing faster. The market for SONET rings, the digital local loops that can automatically fix their own ruptures, is growing about 24 percent a year. And the market for wireless equipment is booming, growing 35 percent to $44 billion in 1996, thanks to subscriber growth, network construction, and the conversion of old analog cellular networks into new digital networks. Merrill Lynch expects the wireless equipment business to grow 24 percent in 1997 and 20 percent in 1998.

Internet Growth

Demand for the Internet is growing at a furious pace. The size of the Internet, measured by the amount of capacity it consumes, doubles every three to four months for an annual increase of 1,000 percent. It's growing for two reasons: More people are going on-line, and they are transmitting increasingly complicated multimedia files that demand bigger information pipes, or higher bandwidth. The problem is that few people have yet figured out a way to make money with the Internet.

About 80 percent of traffic is still devoted to surfing the World Wide Web's free sites, as opposed to buying and selling goods and services, Grubman says. That could change as people place more confidence in the Internet's security against fraud and eavesdropping. "I think use of the Internet for commercial applications could explode in the next few years," Grubman says. Telecommunications companies and Internet access providers could profit from that commercial growth by charging fees to the companies that do business over their networks, much as a landlord collects rent from a retail tenant. It also creates an opportunity for the cyberstores themselves.

The growth of the Internet is also stimulating a booming business in network construction. People are creating new networks much as a commercial developer builds a mall in a growing town on the assumption that new stores will lease the space. An August 1997 report by Credit Suisse First Boston captured this moment in history perfectly:

"Demand does seem insatiable, in much the same way that ever-more-powerful PCs are bought up by consumers," the report says. It describes how WorldCom's chief operating officer, John Sidgmore, told analysts that the company's Internet access unit, UUNet, is facing a severe shortage of capacity. Despite the network construction planned by WorldCom, AT&T, MCI, Sprint, Qwest, IXC, and Vyvx, there wasn't the prospect of a capacity glut anywhere in sight.

"Each one of us contributes to this demand for bandwidth. It's a natural extension of how we use our PCs," CS First Boston says, citing the rising use of e-mail for transmission of huge documents and files. People are no longer willing to wait for a letter or package to arrive by mail or express delivery. They aren't even willing to wait as a fax machine slowly prints a document. "This is grass-roots demand, and we don't think it will diminish anytime soon," the report concludes. "Unlike voice traffic, which has a natural limit, data/Internet traffic doesn't. After all, how fast is fast enough, or how big is big enough, when it comes to your PC? It's increasingly the same thing with the communications link."

The Internet threatens to revolutionize the distribution

The Black Hole in Cyberspace

Cost of Delivery for a 42-page Document			
New York to:	**New York**	**Los Angeles**	**Tokyo**
AT&T (peak)	na	$9.86	$28.83
AT&T (off-peak)	na	$6.88	$28.09
Federal Express	$15.50	$15.50	$26.25
U.S. Mail	$3.00	$3.00	$7.40
NYNEX (peak)	44¢	na	na
NYNEX(off-peak)	16¢	na	na
America Online	6¢	6¢	6¢
Internet	1.4¢	1.4¢	1.4¢

Source: North River Ventures

of goods and services, upsetting the economics of the tele-communications business in the process. North River Ventures published an influential client letter in August 1995 that explains how this works. The investment and consulting firm says the Internet is much cheaper to use than the phone network. That will force traditional carriers to lower prices to levels they can't sustain. The loss of just 6 percent of industry revenue could wipe out all U.S. carriers' profits, North River warned again in October 1997, citing the International Telecommunications Union. Another cause for alarm: Carriers derive a disproportionate amount of profit from international calling, a high-priced realm that is susceptible to raids by cheaper Internet-based networks. "Price pressure like that has the power to swallow carriers whole," North River Partner Francis McInerney says.

Economic Effects of Regulation

As if the economics of the telecommunications industry weren't complicated enough, the entire system has been warped by nearly a century of monopoly regulation. The result is such a muddle that Congress, state regulators, the White House, the FCC, the Justice Department, and the federal courts are unable to develop a clear, workable alternative. This uncertainty has delayed competition between the giants of cable TV and phone service, creating a opening for entrepreneurs to attack the market first. The Kingsbury Agreement of 1911 set a number of social goals for telecommunications: to make the phone as cheap and widely available as possible. The price of basic phone service—a network connection, or dial tone, and cheap local calling—was artificially set by regulators below its actual cost. The local phone companies within AT&T's vast Bell System recouped this subsidy by charging extra for local toll calls. And AT&T's long-distance unit further subsidized the Bell System by charging extra for long-distance calls.

In reality, the phone company doesn't spend appreciably more on a long-distance call than it does on a local call. The real cost is running wires into the ground and connecting people to the system. Once that is done, it doesn't matter if a call goes next door or across the country. If the price of local and long-distance phone service reflected their actual cost, long-distance prices would be much lower, and many local bills would be higher, forcing a significant number of people out of the market.

This system of cross-subsidies reached a new level of complexity when the Bell System was spun off from AT&T in 1984. It was devised around the fact that all long-distance calls begin and end on a local network. The local phone networks serve as on- and off-ramps for calls that travel long-distance. Therefore, long-distance carriers pay a toll for using those ramps, just as motorists pay tolls when they get on and off an interstate highway. Those tolls, known as access charges, are inflated well above the real cost that local phone companies pay for carrying long-distance traffic. Local phone companies say the extra money is used to subsidize cheap local phone service for all residential customers, regardless of their income or where they live. It's generally more expensive to build and operate local networks in rural areas, which means that urban dwellers end up subsidizing rural areas. Businesses also help subsidize local phone service for residential customers. Long-distance companies, which pay the access charges, say the local carriers use the charges to line their pockets.

This complicated system was possible when the local phone business was run by monopolies, but it falls apart in a competitive market. The price of basic local phone service is so low that few people believe they can make money from it unless they have a huge chunk of the local toll market and lots of money from access charges and enhanced services. A newcomer, saddled with heavy start-up costs, will have a difficult time making the business work.

The Telecommunications Act of 1996 tried to unravel this mess and achieve a measure of economic sanity, whereby prices bear some relationship to costs. It ordered the FCC to come up with a new system that would bring phone prices in line with their actual costs and prepare the market for competition. That means cutting access charges, bringing prices in line with costs, and creating a new system to subsidize local phone service for high-cost regions and low-income customers.

Implementing the law has been a nightmare. The access charges generate more than $20 billion a year for the local phone companies. Long-distance companies such as MCI wanted the FCC to cut them by $10 billion, and the local phone companies fought hard to preserve every penny. The FCC came up with a plan in April 1997, after more than a year of fierce lobbying. It cut access charges by $18 billion over five years, raised the price of some local business lines, and created a new mechanism to subsidize local phone service for poor residential customers. It also established a fund to wire libraries, schools, and rural health care facilities for the Internet, as required by the Telecommunications Act. Local phone companies appealed the rules in federal court. The case hasn't been resolved as of this writing, but the local phone carriers have a good track record in court.

GTE successfully appealed an earlier FCC decision that established prices and rules governing the way local carriers open their network to competitors. This issue, known as *interconnection*, stems from the fact that established local phone companies have control over phone numbers, phone lines, billing records, and other crucial aspects of the network. Their competitors need access to all those things when customers switch accounts. The Eighth Circuit Appeals Court ruled in GTE's favor in July 1997 on the grounds that the FCC shouldn't have set rules for the states, which traditionally regulate local phone service. The case is headed to the Supreme Court. Meanwhile, long-distance companies are fuming. They say the local carriers use their control of billing records and other information to sabotage competition. It can take up to three months for a local carrier to switch a competitor over to AT&T or MCI, according to complaints filed with the FCC.

The Bells deny the charges. They say the long-distance companies really don't want to compete in the local market. Once the local markets are competitive, the local phone companies can enter long-distance, which AT&T and MCI fear above all else. GTE and Southern New England Telephone (SNET), the two big local phone companies already in long-distance, have done well against AT&T, MCI, and Sprint. If these lawsuits aren't enough, western local-phone giant SBC Communications has appealed part of the Telecommunications Act itself for good measure. It argues that the law violates the Constitution by keeping the company out of the long-distance market.

These battles have delayed the much-anticipated competition among big companies, leaving an opening for smaller companies. "Since the law will not spark an immediate competitive war in local telephony or cable, that means there will be less pressure than expected for a rapid upgrade of the nation's communications infrastructure," Cleland says. "That also means that the heralded competitive battle between telecom 'super-carriers' over one-stop communications shopping is more than three to four years off, because it depends more on infrastructure upgrades than regulation to become a reality."

Cleland's list of industries that gain an advantage from the slow implementation of the Telecommunications Act is headed by the competitive access providers (CAPs), the entrepreneurial companies that have a head start on the industry giants.

Growth Markets

Network construction

The telecommunications markets of the United States and many other markets across the world are running out of room, and the industry is rushing to build more of them before the current system is swamped. Growing demand for pagers, fax machines, e-mail, Internet access, and other forms of data transmission is growing 35 percent a year. A profusion of new long-distance resellers has also bought excess capacity on the network since the early 1990s. Yet network construction was at a standstill during the mid-1990s despite this rising demand. That pushed capacity utilization on the long-distance network to an all-time high, Salomon Smith Barney analyst Jack Grubman says. A Salomon report in September 1997 said 85 percent of the country's long-distance network is in use at any given moment, far exceeding the optimum level of 65 percent.

One entrepreneur after another agrees: The greatest opportunity in telecommunications today is construction of new high-speed multimedia networks. Entrepreneurs building new networks stand to gain a huge portion of the market. Revenue from local and long-distance phone service will rise 37 percent to $255 billion in 2001, International Data Corp. says.

Competitive local exchange carriers, which held 1.4 percent of the local market in 1997, will capture 8.4 percent of the market by 2001. WorldCom founder and CEO Bernie Ebbers drove the point home on October 1, 1997 as he announced his bid for MCI to a roomful of reporters. Local carriers that lease networks from others achieve margins of

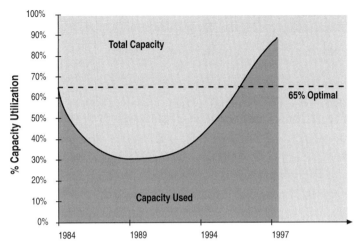

Source: Salomon Smith Barney

Evolution of Capacity Utilization

1984	AT&T, MCI, Sprint, and Wiltel all build fiber networks.
1989	Explosion in long-distance resellers from 100 to 800.
1994	Huge uptick in computer processing power.
	Creation of IP, ATM, on-line services.
	Data growing from below 5% to more than 30% of capacity.
	No new long-haul networks built.
1997	LAN-WAN optical connections.
	Data surpassing voice.

about 20 percent. Carriers that combine leased networks and their own switches boost margins to 40 percent. And those carriers that own their switches and transmission networks have margins of up to 60 percent. That's why Ebbers has made 50 acquisitions in the last five years, acquiring the local networks of MFS, the long-distance networks of Wiltel, and the data networks of UUNet Technologies. As 1997 drew to a close, he was trying to buy MCI.

More entrepreneurs are pouring into the market. Jim Crowe, the former CEO of MFS, is launching into another venture with Peter Kiewit & Sons, which previously owned MFS. It's plan: to build more networks optimized for the Internet and capable of being continually upgraded. Crowe says there is plenty of room for newcomers. "Demand is the least of my worries. You and I will be long gone before the demand for bandwidth stops," he says.

Data transmission and compression

Data is the most quickly growing segment in telecommunications. The U.S. data market will exceed $30 billion in 2000, up from $10 billion in 1996, for a compounded annual growth rate of more than 35 percent, UBS Securities says, citing Yankee Group data. Data growth has been apparent for some time. But the rising importance of the Internet Protocol (IP) sector of the data market became clear in 1997. Internet protocol includes the Internet and related IP technologies such as frame relay and ATM.

"The Internet Protocol market-based market... is fueling the growth of data from new applications, the huge demand for Internet services and greater cost efficiencies," UBS analyst Linda Meltzer said in a November 1997 report prepared for the firm's second annual telecom conference. The IP-based data market should reach $10.5 billion in 2001, up from $2 billion in 1996, she said, citing International Data Corp. That's a 40 percent annual gain. IP networks could take $3 billion in revenue from U.S. carriers by 2001, she said.

IP telephony isn't going to replace the existing network, though, says Chris Lamb, director of business development at 3Com, which makes modems, Internet routers, and other types of equipment. "Tens of trillions of dollars have been invested in the phone network. It isn't going away tomorrow," Lamb says. "If we fast forward 20 or 30 years, phone networks will be a composite of the old and new. We will see new choices."

Data is driving almost all the growth on the long-distance and local networks. Data volume already equals voice traffic on the long-distance network, and it will exceed it within three years. Existing phone networks weren't designed to handle that data traffic. It will take decades to fully replace existing phone networks with high-speed multimedia networks that can accommodate data. Until then, it's crucial to figure out ways of extending the capacity of existing lines through data compression.

"The biggest opportunity to get rich is to invest in a technology that makes revolutionary changes and creates huge efficiencies throughout the network," says Michael Mahoney, portfolio manager of the $2 billion GT Capital Telecommunications Fund. Newbridge Networks and Cisco have earned fortunes in data-networking technology. The next generation of companies to take off could include Amati, Westell, and Paradyne, which have developed technologies that allow phone companies to transmit massive amounts of data over regular copper phone lines. And Lucent Technologies is one of several companies that are compressing data on fiber-optic lines with a new technology called Dense Wavelength Division Multiplexing. Fiber systems have traditionally carried one optical signal per strand. Lucent and other companies are packing multiple color-coded signals into a single fiber strand. That increases capacity to 20 to 40 gigabits a second, up from a standard 2.5 gigabits a second, Lucent says.

Carriers will install high-capacity fiber through much of the network; the problem is increasing the capacity of the copper wires that connect buildings to the fiber network, says Allan Adams, senior vice president at DSC Communications in Dallas. "We're investing our money there, in the last mile," he says. "It's a big area. Entrepreneurs are focusing their money there." The company makes compression equipment such as digital modems, also known as digital subscriber lines. DSL deployment has been somewhat slower than expected, but phone companies will begin rolling out DSL in greater numbers in 1998. Cable companies will begin rolling out cable modems as well.

Lamb of 3Com says these networks will be based on open standards. Carriers won't buy complete networks from a single provider that uses a proprietary standard. They will buy components from various companies that produce interoperable equipment that conforms to open standards.

Internet telephony service providers

The Internet is already drawing traffic away from the voice network, especially in the overpriced international market. Global phone companies could lose $8 billion in revenue to the Internet by 2001, Action Information Services says. One way to tap the market is to become an Internet Telephony Provider, says Dave Goodtree of Forrester Research. It's a relatively inexpensive business to run, with start-up costs in the "tens of thousands of dollars." The business can be launched by reselling the service of a general-purpose Internet-access provider. That eliminates the need to build an Internet Service Provider (ISP) business from scratch. But you will need a partner in each country in which you plan to operate and a local carrier that will complete the calls you carry on your network. The best opportunity for Internet phone service is the international market. Domestic long-distance calls are already relatively cheap, and few people will find it worthwhile to route those calls to the Internet.

Video

As new high-capacity networks and data-compression technologies deliver more bandwidth to the public, video communications will enter the mainstream in the form of video telephony, or video e-mail, and multimedia entertainment. "It will be a camcorder-driven world," says Francis McInerney, partner at North River Ventures, a telecommunications investment and consulting firm. He predicts that video will flow across high-speed networks with the ease that voice flows today. He sees big opportunities at all levels: from network construction to digital compression and routing technologies to the production of multimedia programming. People with film and video production skills will be in demand.

Adams at DSC expects a more gradual transition to video

telephony, which bombed when the local phone companies tried to implement it in the early and mid-1990s. "Let's focus on data first," Adams says. "It's an evolution: voice, data, video."

Consumer markets

Most new carriers target the business market because that where they believe the real spending power lies. "Poppy-cock!" McInerney of North River snorts. "The real opportunity is in the consumer market. It's so much bigger." Consumer spending accounts for about two-thirds of the U.S. economy. The power of the consumer in telecommunications has been muted by a lack of bandwidth to the home. But when that bandwidth arrives, he expects consumer spending to surge. Some new carriers such as RCN and Excel are already targeting the consumer market.

The desktop takes its place in telecommunications

The network has been the repository of telecommunications intelligence. The switching capacity and powerful databases, such as directory services, have always resided on the network, not the "dumb" telephone hanging on the wall of the consumer's home. That balance of power is beginning to change. PBX systems and other small switching systems designed for corporate offices have been around for years. Now the phone itself is getting smart. Sandisk, of Scottsdale, Arizona, is manufacturing postage-stamp size memory cards that slip into wireless phones the way floppy disks fit into a computer. That creates enormous opportunities for entrepreneurs. Possible applications include telephone number directories, or programs that use the memory to record phone conversations or dictation, says Nelson Chan, vice president of marketing. These chips can already hold 30 minutes of voice or up to 1,500 pages of text, he says. Faxes and e-mail can be downloaded and read off line, cutting down on wireless phone costs. Then they can be

SanDisk's MultiMedia Card is expected to add functionality to pagers, mobile phones, and other small handheld systems.

stored for future reference. They also create new opportunities for information services that deliver news, stock quotes, sports scores, and more. "Instead of just receiving a headline, you can receive the story behind the news," Chan says. He predicts that annual sale of smart phones will reach 6 to 7 million by 1999.

Wireless

Two important trends are occurring in wireless. The wireless revolution is spreading from telephones to other devices such as laptop computers and handheld personal digital assistants (PDAs). The greatest growth, though, lies in the gradual replacement of landline phones with wireless phones. AT&T Wireless CEO Dan Hesse says the company is already selling "intrapremise" wireless phones to about 200 corporate clients such as Sony Compact Disk in Eugene, Oregon. Hesse, speaking in December 1997 at Saloman Smith Barney's annual telecommunications conference, said these phones function as cordless phones in office buildings and as wireless phones in other places. They could eliminate the need for regular landline phone service. He expects these devices to gain acceptance among business customers first. But a similar device for consumers is only two or three years away, he says. Wireless carriers report that a small number of consumers—such as young single, urban-dwelling professionals—already make do at home with just a wireless phone. The growth opportunities in wireless are huge for entrepreneurs who have access to the substantial amounts of capital required.

Laptops and other information devices are going wireless, too. 3Com, for example, makes a radio modem that allows people to stay connected to the Internet all the time, receiving e-mail and other information through the Zap It service offered by DTS Wireless in Woodbridge, New Jersey. These modems operate at a slow speed, but they will get faster, says Jeff Abramowitz, wireless marketing manager for 3Com's mobile communications division. The slow speeds are mitigated, he says, because they don't have to dial into the system and retrieve their mail. It arrives unbeknownst to them while they are doing something else.

Global telecommunications

The key to telecom demand is economic growth, and over the next decade, most of the world's economic growth will take place outside of the United States, says David Roddy, chief telecommunications economist at Deloitte & Touche Consulting Group. Growth in the Asia-Pacific region will be at least four times as fast as U.S. growth by the year 2000, Roddy wrote in a research report in February 1997.

"We believe that telecommunications is the key driver of rapid economic development. Landline, wireless, and video information technology have as much potential to create change in the global economy as mass-market manufacturing did in the Western world at the beginning of the Industrial Revolution," Roddy says. "For businesses in telecommunications and related industries, the opportunities are significant." The opportunities lie in bringing telecommunications to high-growth regions that don't have enough phones. Roddy notes that half the world's population has never made a telephone call. North America has 30 percent of the world's phone lines and only 10 percent of its population. The Asia-Pacific region has 60 percent of global population and only 20 percent of the phone lines.

The barriers to entry are high. The cost and difficulty of network construction is compounded by other challenges. Global telecom entrepreneurs must have fluent understanding of the languages and cultures of the countries in which they plan to operate.

An easier route into the global market is to provide a call-back service in countries with high international rates. Callers in these countries dial a toll-free number in the United States. They hang up after the first ring and wait for the call-back company to return the call, providing a lower-cost U.S. dial tone. The service is illegal in some countries. It can be immensely profitable, but the margins will fade as international rates begin to decline. Call-back pioneers such as USA Global Link are already diversifying into new lines of business such as Internet telephony.

Wholesale

There are close to 1,000 long-distance carriers in the United States, up from one in the 1960s. New competitors are pouring into the wireless market, and the local market is about to see an invasion of new companies, too. Most of these new carriers buy their service from larger carriers at wholesale rates and resell it to the public at a competitive price. That's creating a new opportunity for large and small network-based carriers to sell service to other carriers. "Wholesale is by far the fastest growing part of the industry," Excel CEO Kenny Troutt says. "It's 25–30 percent of sales at Frontier, WorldCom, and LCI."

Web hosting

Many companies lack the money or expertise to maintain their own 24-hour-a-day connection to the Internet, so they lease computers and Internet connections from other companies, such as Internet service providers. There are plenty of Web-hosting services in the world, but few of them are good, says David Goodtree of Forrester Research. There's a lot of opportunity, but it isn't a cheap business. Start-up costs can run into millions of dollars. Companies that attempt to enter the market on a shoestring budget run into problems, Goodtree says. Another source of trouble: Many Web-hosting services combine their business with Web page design. "You probably don't want to compete with the Web design business," Goodtree says. "The skills are entirely different. One business is about guys in ponytails; the other is about computer rooms."

Web-hosting services must provide 24-hour-a-day, seven-day-a-week customer service. Equipment costs include routers, switches, and racks of servers (the computers that store clients' Web sites). The system must be connected to an Internet backbone service and one or two backup services. Staff must include Unix computer gurus and a sales force. The computers must be stored in an air-conditioned room with a raised floor to keep cables out of harm's way. The entire operation must be protected behind secure doors.

Security monitoring

The Telecommunications Act of 1996 was a boon for an often-overlooked sector of the market: security monitoring. "The most under-appreciated tele-theme to emerge from the new law… is bringing economies of scale to the remote monitoring industry," says Scott Cleland, now director of the Precursor Group at Legg Mason.

Many industries have long-used telecom networks to monitor their operations across a broad geographic area. Cleland cites several examples: Utilities have used telecommunications to monitor network performance and customer usage. Home-security companies have monitored alarms, trucking companies have monitored their fleets, vending machine companies have monitored inventories of candy bars and soft drinks, and shipping companies such as UPS and FedEx have monitored the delivery of packages. "Out of necessity and in search of increased productivity, companies have individually pioneered their own specialized remote-monitoring networks," Cleland says. "This is a highly inefficient use of resources."

Several conditions are spurring the creation of new companies that will specialize in remote monitoring. The Telecommunications Act forces the Bells to open their network to competitors, giving monitoring companies a direct connection to consumers. The rise of the Internet creates a cheap, universal network that can be used for monitoring. And the FCC's sale of a huge amount of radio spectrum creates more capacity for wireless carriers that can specialize in monitoring.

Home network integration

The demand for network integration is enormous. The variations are endless. Old databases designed for mainframe computers must be integrated with the new world of the Internet. Computer systems will soon be integrated with cable and satellite television services. A growing number of PCs are already cable-ready, just as televisions are. Many small companies already help businesses tie their communications into a coherent network. Consumers will soon need similar services for their homes. "People need to wire their homes," says Judy Reed Smith, president of Atlantic/ ACM, a Boston consulting firm. "We have four computers and a printer that had to be networked together." She hired a contractor, Massachusetts Telecommunications Associates, to build a household network when she moved into a new home in 1997.

Convergence of power companies and telecommunications

Both industries are based on networks. Both industries have undergone rapid revision of old monopoly rules. Now they are quickly converging. RCN Communications is offering telecommunications over power utility networks in Washington and Boston. Northern Telecom, Ltd., a telecommunications company based in Canada, is offering Internet access in England in a partnership with United Utilities PLC, a power company. The power lines provide access to the Internet ten times faster than a phone line. The power and the data signal are split by a box attached to a meter. The data signal and the electricity are carried from the meter into the home by separate cables.

Education and consulting

"There is tremendous opportunity to educate people who don't know how to get started," says Matthew Howard, a marketing executive at Vertical Networks, a Silicon Valley start-up. A few examples: Forrester Research, The Yankee Group, and Jupiter Communications have developed highly successful businesses tracking consumer trends in the world of the network. Forrester Research is rumored to be considering an initial public offering. TeleChoice has specialized in such new technologies as high-speed phone lines that carry voice, video, and data. Consumers and small businesses turn to books and consulting firms to help them sift through the bewildering number of alternatives for satellite service, wireless phone service, and computing. These choices are increasingly important because more people are working from home at least part-time.

Rooftop rights

Some major cities will soon have as many as eight wireless phone networks operating within their borders. Where will all those antennas go? Suitable sites are a scare commodity. The geographic conditions must be right, and the frequent objections of local property owners and zoning commissions must be overcome. Several companies are specializing in winning antenna rights to roofs and hilltops and reselling them to wireless carriers. It's one of the hottest ancillary industries spawned by wireless technology.

Content

As network construction proceeds at a blistering pace, companies must fill them up with radio, television, and Internet transmissions; Web-based stores; and news and information services. Anyone can learn to construct a Web page in a few minutes, but the original, useful, and hard-to-duplicate services are in great demand. A few examples: PointCast and Yahoo, which transmit custom news reports over the Web, and Amazon.com, the Web-based bookseller.

Fax

The fax machine might seem passé in the world of e-mail and the Internet, but it's not. "It will be a long time before e-mail has a serious impact on the fax," says Dave Friend, founder of FaxNet. He says the fax market is growing 20 percent a year. WorldCom's UUNet Technologies unit estimates that the market is worth $60 billion a year in revenue. UUNet and other carriers are routing fax traffic from phone lines to the Internet. That's lowering the cost of sending a fax, which is likely to spur even more growth. Fax machines have become a standard form of communication for businesses—and even consumers—around the world. Fax users far exceed e-mail users, and they will for some time, Friend says.

Equipment

The multi-billion market for transmission equipment, switches, access technologies, and phones is growing around the world. Equipment makers such as Lucent are among the stars of the stock market. There are many niches that these companies can't fill: antenna towers, sheds that conceal and protect equipment in the field, shelves for stacking switches, and computer monitors in the central office.

Up-and-Coming Niches

Prepaid local and wireless

The prepaid calling card turned into a multi-billion-dollar niche within the long-distance business, and that success is about to be duplicated in the local and wireless sectors. The prepaid wireless market generated $750 million in revenue in 1997, and it could grow several hundred billion dollars a year for the next few years, says Eric Stebel, associate publisher of Multimedia Publishing in Houston, which publishes *Telecom Business*.

It's an easy business to enter: Simply buy wireless debit phones for about $200 a piece, and resell them for what the market will bear. They are available from five companies, starting at $188 each. Vendors are Telemac, Omni Communications, JRC Canada, Topp Telecom, and US/Intellicom. There are several variations on the technology. Debit phones can be programmed with a certain number of prepaid minutes. Customers can purchase additional time

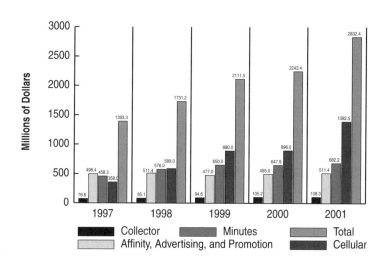

Prepaid Cards and Calling: The Forecast
Source: The Yankee Group, 1997

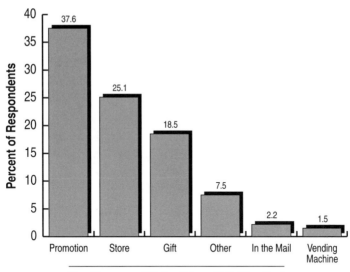

How Consumer Obtained Prepaid Calling Card

Source: The Yankee Group, 1977

by returning to the store where they bought their phone. They can also buy a prepaid cellular calling card that entitles them to use the phone for a certain amount of time.

Target markets include people who have credit problems and can't qualify for standard cellular service. And PCS (Personal Communications Service) phones that use GSM (Global Standard for Mobile communication) technology accept smart cards that can be programmed for a certain amount of time. GSM phones lend themselves to a related application: sharing phones. An employer can distribute cards to a group of workers, allowing them to share phones. They simply install their smart card when they want to use it.

Prepaid local service barely exists today, but Stebel expects it to be a $500-million-a-year market by 2002. It is targeted toward the 2 percent of the population that can't qualify for standard phone service because of bad credit or a complete lack of credit history. Prepaid local customers can make unlimited local, toll-free, and 911 calls. They can also purchase enhanced services such as Caller ID. But they do not get access to live operators or directory assistance.

Note: Prepaid local service providers must be authorized by state regulators before they go into business.

"If I was going to go into telecommunications right now, I'd do prepaid local," Stebel says. "It's such a huge market, and it's not that difficult to do." Start-up costs for a carrier that wants to operate in a single state are probably in the tens of thousands of dollars. The biggest costs are certification and marketing. And prepaid services allow the carrier to receive payment up-front, reducing the credit risk and cash flow problems that plague many conventional carriers.

Flat-rate long-distance pay phones

Another emerging niche is flat-rate, long-distance phone service for pay phones, Stebel says. They allow callers to call any number in the U.S. for a flat rate, often 25 cents a minute. A good source of information is *Payphone Magazine*.

Wireless for businesses

Most wireless companies market to businesses the same way they market to consumers, says David Goodtree of Forrester Research. They are making a big mistake. Businesses have different needs. They require account managers, 24-hour service, and instant replacement of broken equipment. The market has room for new wireless businesses that cater directly to those commercial customers. Few carriers are doing it today.

Things That Need Inventing

E-mail fulfillment bureau

Just as L.L. Bean and other catalog companies hire a third party to manage their huge, nationwide mailings, Goodtree says there's a need for a new kind of company to manage mass e-mail transmissions for retailers sprouting up on the Web. One company, called Axiom, is already a pioneer in this market. An e-mail fulfillment house needs long lists of consumers, complete with name and e-mail address, that it can sell to marketing firms. It will also handle the nuts and bolts of a mass mailing, addressing the mail, tracking it during transmission, and possibly even filling orders for goods and services.

Putting communications devices into new environments

Telecommunications devices encompass much more than the telephone these days. Automatic teller machines and credit-card verification machines employ phone lines. Next, we'll see vending machines automatically send a message over the phone line to the supplier, announcing that inventory is running low. Many new services can be created by a simple act of systems integration, combining a communications device and a computer chip with an infinite variety of objects:

Global positioning systems (GPS): Global positioning devices are cheap, and they can be imbedded almost anywhere. "You can walk into an REI store and buy a handheld GPS device for a couple of hundred bucks," Goodtree says. These satellite-based devices transmit signals that are coordinated with a mapping system, identifying the location of the transmitter.

Smart pagers: Let's say a household oil tank is nearly empty. A flow-meter could be programmed to trigger a pager when the tank is running low, summoning the oil company to refill it.

Jobs in Demand

Radio frequency engineers

The wireless industry needs behind-the-scenes technicians to build and maintain wireless antenna networks, says Jerry Dotson, director of technical education at AT&T Wireless Services. The industry will need 250,000 of them by 2005, up from just 25,000 in 1997, he says. Seattle Central Community College, based near AT&T Wireless headquarters in Kirkland, Washington, has created a two-year program in Wireless Communications to help train people for these jobs. Classes are half theory, half application.

Router jocks for hire

The growing importance of the Internet has created sudden demand for engineers who can run these networks. There's a particular need for technicians trained to operate Cisco routers, the computers that direct packets of information across the Internet, says analyst David Goodtree of Forrester Research. International Network Services, a publicly held company, has already made inroads into this booming market. The company dispatches its Cisco-certified engineers to corporations around the world. They earn $100,000 a year designing, building, and managing Internets and Intranets for Internet service providers. The demand for "router jocks for hire" will continue to rise. "This is a many-year problem," Goodtree says. The start-up costs are limited to recruitment, which will include a signing bonus and training at Cisco.

Java programmers

"Java programming is hot. There is tremendous opportunity for software development. It is probably the easiest place for an entrepreneur to find an opportunity," says Matthew Howard, a marketing executive with Vertical Networks, a Silicon Valley start-up that is creating switching technology for multimedia networks. Many Web sites are enlivened with little pieces of Java animation, and that's just the beginning of what the programming language can do. It's playing an increasingly important role, for example, in the creation of data warehouses. Sun Microsystems trains and certifies people as Java programmers and developers, who easily earn $75 to $125 an hour. The programmer test, which costs $150, is available by calling Sun Educational Services at 800-422-8020. People who pass the programmer test can advance to the developer level by completing a programming assignment and taking a second $150 test. "Demand is insatiable," Howard says.

Overlooked or Underrated Markets

Telecom service agents, distributors

Operating largely beyond the gaze of government regulators, the business press, and the investment community, agents and distributors make their way in the telecom market by selling the service of local, long-distance, and wireless carriers. Nearly all carriers hire individuals and small, privately owned companies on a contract basis to supplement the full-time sales forces.

Unlike telecom resellers, agents and distributors do not require government authorization to sell their wares. They are selling someone else's service, not their own. And unlike resellers, agents and distributors do not compete with the carriers that supply the products they sell. They are allies, and they often achieve better margins than resellers do. The big difference between an agent and a distributor is that the latter often has a back office and a support staff. Distributors often agree to sell a minimum volume of phone service in a given month. If they don't meet the quota, they can be held responsible for the balance. In exchange, distributors often receive a deeper discount than an agent. They might be able to buy long-distance service at 8 cents a minute instead of 9 cents, for example.

Agents and distributors don't need to raise funds in the capital markets or report their earnings to the public. They don't need regulatory approval, and they are too small to get the attention of the mainstream press. They are ignored by all, except industry insiders, customers, and the trade press. Yet this multi-billion-dollar sector of the telecommunications market is a veritable hothouse of entrepreneurism.

"The RBOCs (Regional Bell Operating Companies) take their largest (distributors) and give them better rates than they can get through resale… It's more favorable than being a reseller by far," says Denis Raue, president of Telegration, a long-distance reseller, agent, and distributor in Troy, Michigan. His margins as a distributor of Ameritech's local service are as high as 20 percent. Ameritech offers resellers discount margins of about 25 percent, but distributors don't face the same steep investments.

There are numerous entry points to the market. All major carriers and many second- and third-tier resellers hire agents and distributors. Many smaller carriers advertise programs for agents and distributors in the pages of such trade journals as *Telecom Business*. Some resellers, such as Unidial, conduct all of their sales through agents and distributors. They are selective, but they will invest tens of thousands of dollars to train and support them.

A would-be distributor must convince a carrier that he has a good business plan and a solid financial background. Distributors may need $250,000 to set up an office and pay sales people in advance. The business plan must demonstrate a ready pool of customers. It can be based on the everyday experience that most people gather while building a career or participating in a community group. Someone with experience in the hotel or locksmith industry, for example, might figure out a way to market telecommunications service to those contacts from a prior career.

Reselling phone services

Resale of local phone service is not economically viable, the critics say. Potential competitors in the local phone market demanded 30 to 40 percent discounts from the regional Bells and GTE. Government-arbitrated negotiations have produced discounts in the 20 percent range. AT&T, MCI, and a host of analysts say 20 percent simply isn't enough to cover capital costs and marketing, while producing a reasonable profit.

They are right and wrong. It's difficult to make money in the local resale market as it is currently structured in many markets across the country. A few intrepid entrepreneurs are betting that the margins in the local resale business will improve, though. "I think the local phone business is probably going to be our most powerful product," says Kenny Troutt, founder of number-five-ranked long-distance carrier Excel. His route into the local market will be the same as his route into long-distance: resale. "I'm not saying it's a good product today… We still have to work out provisioning and continue to negotiate a better price. But I think we will see it happen, just like in long-distance."

The optimists include Michael Mahoney, portfolio manager of GT Capital's $2 billion telecommunications fund, the largest telecom fund in the world. Margins will improve for three reasons, he says. The first reason is that entrepreneurs will cut costs in radical ways, making the most of existing margins. Tel-Save, for example, has established a precedent in the long-distance market, where it advertises via America Online. It buys its service for about 7 cents a minute, mostly from AT&T. Its marketing costs are about half a cent a minute, which is less than the marketing costs incurred by big carriers that advertise on prime-time television. It resells long-distance service in the 9- to 11-cent-a-minute range, which leaves room for a healthy margin. Similar scenarios could make local resale more profitable, Mahoney says.

The second reason is that margins will also start to improve as the regional Bells and GTE face increasing competition from start-up carriers with their own local fiber networks. These companies will begin to view resellers more as allies. It's preferable to share revenue with a reseller who uses their network rather than lose an account to a competing network. Carriers will offer resellers better deals.

Thirdly, entrepreneurs will venture into a form of partial resale that allows them to use their own limited switches and network elements and lease what they don't have from another carrier. WorldCom CEO Bernie Ebbers says this form of resale raises margins to about 40 percent. "Resale has got a lot of potential to be successful, but it's going to take some time," Mahoney says.

Resale is, in fact, quickly spreading from long-distance to the local and wireless markets. Close to 1,000 resellers already exist in the United States, and the number will grow as new markets are created. Their ranks include small companies and powerful carriers such as AT&T, which is reselling local service, and MCI, which is reselling local and wireless. Some of these companies simply purchase a service from another carrier and resell it under their own name. Others buy or lease elements of another carrier's network, but maintain their own switches and transmission equipment.

Resale allows a company quick access to the market with a minimal investment in equipment and infrastructure. Several billion-dollar-a-year companies have risen from the ranks of long-distance resellers. They have taken customers from AT&T, MCI, and Sprint, and forced these telecom giants to change their marketing tactics. Yet for all its success, resale has its limits. A company that has the resources to build and manage its own network often makes more money over the long-term.

Resale places unique demands on the entrepreneur's ability to negotiate a good deal. Resale can be viewed as a form of arbitrage. The reseller exists because a product can simultaneously have a different price in two markets. The reseller buys phone service in the wholesale market and re-sells it, at a slightly higher price, in the retail market. This is not unlike a currency trader buying Swiss francs in one market and selling them seconds later in another country where the price is momentarily higher. It isn't pure arbitrage, though. A Swiss franc is a Swiss franc no matter who sells it, but a telecommunications company can differentiate even a resold product through marketing, customer service, or special features.

The reseller's margins are based on its ability to buy service at the cheapest possible wholesale price. The wholesale rates for long-distance service vary depending on the volume of the purchase, says Gene Chase, founder of long-distance reseller Pantel, with about 40,000 customers in 46 states.

"Somewhere in the 8-cent range would be aggressive at the wholesale level," says Chase, who focuses on the residential market.

It takes a big company to get a really low price on long-distance service these days, says Kenny Troutt, founder of the giant reseller Excel. A $10,000 contract was big enough to get the best-available price when Excel was founded in the late 1980s. Today a reseller has to place an order worth $1 billion to get the best price.

Price isn't always the ultimate driver, Chase says. Consumers don't always choose their long-distance carrier solely on the basis of price, and resellers don't either. He recommends that resellers follow these seven principles as they negotiate contracts:

* Don't rely on a single carrier. Buy your service from two or three. You must have a backup if your relationship with one carrier sours, if its service deteriorates, or if it goes out of business. Chase recommends having several carriers at once to help you negotiate better contracts. About one-third of resellers have three underlying carriers, according to the Telecommunications Resellers Association. About one-fifth of them use four carriers; about 20 percent, more than four.

* Pay attention to the terms of payment. How quickly must the carrier fulfill an order? Your customers should start receiving service from you in three to five days. Can your underlying carrier provide service that quickly?

* Make sure the carrier is highly automated. Can it accommodate larger orders or special requests for service?

⊡ Make sure the carrier is financially stable. Chase looks for suppliers with at least $50 million to $100 million in revenue.

⊡ Make sure the carrier allows you to monitor the progress of orders you have placed.

⊡ Determine exactly how much deposit will be required. Some carriers require an escrow fund with 60 days worth of payments.

⊡ Look for carriers that will provide you with daily call records. Monthly call records aren't sufficient.

Quickest, Cheapest Route into Telecom

For the entrepreneur on a really low budget, Amway offers what appears to be the most inexpensive telecom play. The household and beauty products distributor also markets MCI service. People can become Amway representatives by purchasing a $151 business kit that entitles them to sell MCI service.

Amway-MCI's phone number is 800-926-9293.

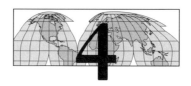

Systems

Most people in the United States take the telephone system for granted. About 94 percent of U.S. households have a phone, and local service is cheap with a standard for reliability that few technologies can match. If we want to speak with someone across town, across the continent, or on the other side of the world, we can pick up the phone with almost complete assurance that our call will be successful.

Drivers aren't particularly surprised if the car fails to start on a harsh winter morning. Office workers have developed a certain cynicism about the reliability of copying machines and computer networks. Many travelers refuse to place their well-being in the hands of an airline. But these same people expect their phone to work, to always be there like the sun or the moon. It's woven into every aspect of life, from the trivialities of gossip to the gravest matters of public safety, with a success rate that exceeds 99 percent.

This chapter explains how the process works. It examines some of the basic components of the traditional telephone network and various devices that tap into it, from the standard telephone to the cellular phone and the satellite phone. It also examines some of the costs of building a network, or leasing someone else's.

Making a Call

Making phone calls are the same as in Bell's day: An electromagnetic microphone converts the differences in acoustical pressure (sound waves) into comparable differences in electrical signal amplitudes. Those differences travel across a copper wire to another telephone, which converts the electrical signals back into sound waves that are emitted through a small speaker. A computer known as a switch assigns an open circuit, or wire, for each call, and makes sure it arrives at the proper destination.

Phone calls travel across a twisted pair of copper wires which is capable of carrying a two-way conversation. It travels a short distance along this thin strand to a collection point known as a *multiplexer*. This device combines lots of calls into a much fatter pipe that can hold dozens, or hundreds, of conversations at once. It's like a traffic interchange where dozens of local streets feed into a highway.

The smallest collection point—known as a T1 line—can carry the equivalent of 24 phone lines. One T1 line might serve about 200 customers in a high-rise apartment building or on a street lined with homes. The network doesn't need a separate circuit for each customer, because it's rare that everyone connected to a single T1 line is using their phone at the same time. But if there aren't enough T1 lines, some customers will get an annoying message, telling them all circuits are busy and to try their call later. The call can travel over a T1 line for a mile or two without losing strength, but it must be boosted to travel longer distances. That's one reason that rural markets are more expensive to serve—they require more equipment in the network.

The T1 line carries the call to a local phone company's central office, where two important things occur. The T1 line feeds into a larger capacity transmission line. It's like the point where a state highway feeds into an interstate highway. This interstate highway carries the equivalent of 28 T1 lines, or 672 phone calls. It's known as a T3 or a DS3. The call is also processed by a computer known as a switch, which routes calls to their destination.

The DS3 line will feed into even wider transmission lines. The DS3 line might also feed into a digital transmission line with much greater capacity. Many local networks use optical transmission lines known as Synchronous Optical Network (SONET) rings. In addition to their enormous capacity for carrying calls, they also have separate channels that carry information about the performance of the network. This allows the phone company to instantly reroute a call if the SONET ring is broken.

The central office also contains computers known as switches, which route the call to its final destination, handing it off to a long-distance carrier if necessary.

There are many variations on this basic design, many of which increase the capacity of the copper wire that connects a phone line to the T1 line or the central office. The phone network has enormous capacity on major transmission routes. The big question is how to increase the capacity of the thin copper wires that connect to the customer's phone. It's impossible to deliver high-speed data or video services without a high-capacity connection to the customer's home. Networks must be reconstructed to replace or enhance the so-called last mile of copper in the network, the distance between the customer and the nearest multiplexing equipment in the network.

The financial rewards of owning switches, transmission equipment, and fiber are enormous. The cash-flow margins for local phone companies that own their complete network are about 45 percent, although owners have to make huge investments to achieve those margins. The margins for local phone companies that buy local service from another carrier and resell it to the public are much lower, although the initial investments are lower, too.

Building Local Networks

Building a local network from scratch—including the switches, transmission equipment, and phone lines in the ground—costs about $4,000 per customer in initial investments, says Don LaChance, a senior product manager at switch-maker Summa Four. The costs drop to $3,000 per customer for companies that lease local transmission lines, he adds. LaChance, a veteran of Boston Technologies and Northern Telecom, says its costs about $1,000 a subscriber to construct a long-distance network.

AT&T reports that total service resale costs the company an average $14.81 per line each month in payments to the local phone company, and that the business produces $20 per line in revenue. The costs of building a nationwide local network from scratch are enormous. Legg Mason Wood Walker, a brokerage firm based in Baltimore, says the nation's local phone companies have networks worth $270 billion. Fortunately, there is a compromise between the costly-but-profitable and the inexpensive-but-unprofitable extremes. The Telecommunications Act forces big local phone companies to resell their networks on an unbundled basis as well. That is, a competitor with its own switches or transmission equipment can lease what it needs from the local carrier and no more. AT&T says the average unbundled line will cost the company $16.03 a month per line in payments to the local phone company and produce $33.50 in revenue. The margins will differ from one company to another, depending on how much of its own equipment it can afford to buy and what sort of bulk price it can command. Yet the margins are almost always better in unbundled resale, provided one can afford the initial investment.

Many companies, including AT&T, MCI, and RCN, are using total-service resale to gain quick entry to the local market, and converting service to their own lines or unbundled lines as they grow.

The price of transmission and switching equipment

varies wildly. The cost is tied to the number of phone lines it accommodates, the number of enhanced features it has programmed into it, or the nature of its data ports. "There are so many variables, there is no one answer to the question of price," says Bob Papek, of Allied Communications, an equipment vendor in Council Bluffs, Iowa. The company sells transmission equipment to small independent phone companies and other businesses, such as railroads and energy pipeline companies, that want to build private communications networks. About 90 percent of the company's inventory is used. Most of its customers are looking for systems that handle from 1,000 to 10,000 phone lines.

A rule of thumb for pricing used switches and transmission equipment: Plan to spend about $100 for every phone line that the switch or multiplexer can handle, Papek says. That means that a 5,000-line switch would cost about $500,000. Remember, though, that switching and transmission equipment doesn't need to accommodate every single customer on a network; they won't all talk at once. The $100-a-line rule is a rough estimate for a basic Class-Five switch, which are produced by major manufacturers such as Lucent and Northern Telecom.

Some networks will deploy a basic Class-Five switch for routing traffic, and install another switch to manage and deploy enhanced services such as caller ID and call forwarding. Summa Four, based near Boston, has developed a unique two-part programmable switch, which is used by many medium-to-large telecommunications companies. One part interacts with the phone network, while a separate unit, such as a PC, is used to program and control the switch and its special calling features. It's a tool for creating custom-calling features. The Summa Four switch reflects the increasing integration of the computer and the telephone and the opportunities that are available to the creative entrepreneur.

Summa Four's lowest-priced switch would cost $40,000 to $50,000, but it would handle only about 100 lines. A basic switch that accommodates 500 to 1,000 lines would cost $300,000 or $400,000. Switches that handle 5,000 to 10,000 lines typically cost $400 a line. But the incremental cost begins to fall beyond that point, Papek says. The incremental cost for a switch with 20,000 lines might be $200 a line, he adds.

The building blocks of these services include voice-mail, caller-ID, and voice-recognition systems. A voice-mail system can be constructed for $2,000 to $3,000 a port, says LaChance, of Summa Four. A port can accommodate about 300 mail boxes. An interactive voice response system costs closer to $1,000 for a single phone line. These are the systems that allow people to navigate through their bank's automated information line, responding to voice prompts with a touch-tone keypad, although the applications are getting more sophisticated every year. Interactive voice response systems are the basis for digital assistants that integrate e-mail, voice-mail, and faxes in a single mailbox. The system can convert an e-mail message into a voice message and read it over the phone, or it can convert a voice-mail message into a fax and send it to a computer. Wildfire Communications, TPS Call Sciences, and other "digital assistants" will answer a phone with a recorded message, put the caller on hold, and track the customer down at home, in the office, or on the road. The phone, the computer, and the Internet will gradually merge until they are indistinguishable, LaChance says. "It will take 30 years to really accomplish this," he adds.

The Telephone Network in Transition

In the meantime, the basic phone network is already in a huge transition. The long-distance network already consists of high-speed fiber transmission lines, and the local network is just beginning to catch up. There are numerous alternatives to the standard copper wire connection between the customer and the main trunks of the local network. Several new technologies send higher-speed digital transmissions over the existing copper wire. They are identified with an alphabet soup of acronyms: ISDN, HDSL, ADSL, and ATM, plus frame relay. The copper can also be replaced with fiber-optic cable and coaxial cable to create a combination known as *hybrid-fiber coax*.

There's an increasing array of wireless options. Cellular phones and Personal Communications Services (PCS) are wireless alternatives to the traditional phone and the copper connection. They use small radios and antennas planted on the ground or on a roof to connect voice and data to the local network central offices. And within several years, space-based satellite systems will carry an increasing amount of voice and data for businesses and even consumers. All of these options, from ISDN to space-based satellites, can be thought of as alternatives to the telephone's traditional local copper tether. They introduce new elements of high speed or mobility, or both.

ISDN (integrated services digital network)

This is a data service that transmits digital information over a copper line at 128 kilobits a second. It's ten times faster than a 28.8 modem, which makes it adequate for retrieving text and some graphics and video from the Internet, but it isn't fast enough to support live video. Customers must buy special pieces of equipment that attach their computer modems to the phone line. These devices allow customers to make phone calls and receive faxes or data transmissions at the same time. Each ISDN line requires two modems: one in the network and one on the customer's computer. They cost several hundred dollars each, but the customer pays for only one of them.

ADSL (asynchronous digital subscriber line)

This allows transmission of digital video and data in one direction over a regular copper line at relatively high speed of 1.5 megabits a second, which is on par with a TI line. Information from the network to the user moves much faster than information from the user back to the network. Hence, it's designation as an asynchronous system.

HDSL (high speed digital subscriber line)

This is similar to ADSL, but it sends information at high speed in both directions, at 6 megabits a second or faster. At faster speeds, it's suitable for live two-way video transmission. Bell Atlantic, US West, SBC, and other big local phone companies plan to introduce the service on a commercial basis in 1998.

Frame relay

This is a data service that operates at speeds up to 12.2 megabits a second. It was designed to carry just data, but it is carrying voice now as well. It creates something called a virtual circuit. Instead of creating an exclusive connection or circuit between two phone lines, frame relay systems create a defined path through a shared network.

ATM (asynchronous transfer mode)

This is a high-speed transmission line that carries two-way voice, video, and data at super-high speed over a combination of copper and fiber. The current speed limit of 155 megabits a second will soon be exceeded by a 622 megabit version. ATM uses a form of packet switching, as the Internet does, that breaks information into packets of 53 bytes each. Five of the bytes are reserved for routing information. This allows packets from numerous different phone calls and data transmissions to share the same circuit without getting lost or interfering with each other. ATM can be used for public or private networks, like the Internet, but it has enough capacity for live, two-way full-motion video. The U.S. Government is funding the a wireless ATM system known as the Mobile Information Infrastructure Project. The idea is to create a nationwide wireless network that allows people to send and receive multimedia data with wireless laptop computers.

Fiber

The phone network will ultimately be reconstructed as an all-fiber system that carries voice, video, and data—although the transition will take far longer than the phone companies predicted in the early 1990s. Bell Atlantic has installed just such as system in Toms River, New Jersey. It operates on a commercial basis, and it competes with the local cable company, but on a small scale. The construction of these networks slowed down as cable companies scaled back their plans to enter the phone business. But Bell Atlantic says its still intends to have a full-service fiber-optic network available in Philadelphia in 1998. The Toms River system was operated as an open dial-tone system, meaning that the government didn't subject it to cable regulations because it carried a number of competing video systems. But phone companies may choose to operate as regulated cable companies in the future, allowing them exclusive use of their networks, Price Waterhouse says.

Cable systems

Cable television systems are scaling back their efforts to offer telephone service, but they are moving into high-speed Internet access. Manufacturers couldn't develop cable modems as fast as they expected, but the deployment is finally beginning. Cable modems can transmit data at 40 megabits a second. Some systems can achieve that speed in two directions. That's fast enough to accommodate live two-way, full-motion video, but the capacity is limited because lots of customers share the same transmission line. If everyone connected to a transmission line tries to go on-line at once, a capacity shortage can develop. Cable companies are also rebuilding their networks with fiber optic lines that can handle digital transmissions. That will transform the cable system into a two-way communications system offering more television channels, phone service, video on demand, and high-speed Internet access.

The Growth of Wireless

The wireless phone has penetrated between 12 percent and 17 percent of the U.S. population since the first commercial cellular phones were deployed in Chicago in the mid-1980s. There are 50 to 60 million wireless subscribers in the United States, and that number is expected to double by 2000. As prices drop, wireless phones will become an increasingly viable alternative to the traditional wired phone. The wireless phone is a handheld two-way radio that sends voice and data to an antenna that serves a 2- to 25-mile region known as a *cell*. The antenna connects the wireless network to the local network at the central-office level.

By 1998, a new generation of digital wireless phones known as Personal Communications Services (PCS) will account for one-third of the wireless market in the United States. The FCC has licensed up to six PCS carriers in each market. PCS is similar to cellular, although it operates at different frequencies. PCS operates at 1900 megahertz, while cellular operates at 800 megahertz. PCS networks use smaller cells, which allows them to use lighter, longer-lasting batteries. PCS systems can also be broken up into tiny networks of one cell each, opening up a huge opportunity for the entrepreneur who wants to provide specialized services to college campuses, health facilities, corporate campuses, or even single buildings.

PCS companies use a variety of currently incompatible digital technologies. AT&T, for example, uses Time Division Multiple Access (TDMA), which carries three to six conversations on a single channel. Analog cellular systems carry only one conversation per channel. Sprint PCS is using a technology known as CDMA, or Code Division Multiple Access, which carries up to ten conversations per channel. GSM, with 20 million users abroad, is a European version of TDMA. GSM phones also accept so-called smart cards, which can customize a single phone with such features as additional phone numbers, which allows the same phone to be used by different people.

Wireless phones are nearly synonymous with portable, handheld phones, but that may soon change. AT&T is experimenting in Chicago with a fixed wireless system. Users will place a pizza-box-sized antenna on the roof or side of their home, which will connect to a wired or cordless phone inside their home. The system can be used to bypass the traditional local phone network, allowing AT&T to better compete with the established local phone companies. Other companies, such as WinStar, have also developed versions of fixed wireless technology.

Two-way wireless technology has also been synonymous with voice communications, although that definition may be expanding as well. The first recent attempt to develop a wireless video system was known as Multi-channel Multi-point Distribution System (MMDS) or, even more simply, as wireless cable. It has been used as an alternative to cable television. The analog version carries only 33 channels. Bell Atlantic and the old independent incarnations of Pacific Telesis and Nynex had planned to deploy a digital version that carries more channels, but dropped the plan. MMDS is prone to interference and requires a clear line of sight, and only 80 percent of homes in a given region can use it under the best of circumstances, according to Price Waterhouse.

The FCC is preparing to issue licenses for a similar technology known as Local Multipoint Distribution Service (LMDS). CellularVision, which invented the technology, claims that its system has vastly more capacity and solves the line-of-sight problem as well. Its antennas are only half the height of MMDS antennas, and the receiving dishes are small. The dishes are shaped like oversized rearview mirrors and can be placed inside a customer's window. CellularVision describes the technology as "fiber in the sky" and says it will be able to carry two-way voice, video, and high-speed data.

The Next Wave: Satellites

The next wave in wireless communications is the satellite. Once the exclusive tool of governments and major corporations, the $10 billion satellite industry could triple during the next decade, Price Waterhouse says. The market includes three quickly growing sectors. Very Small Aperture Terminals (VSATs) are used for corporate data networking and telecommunications in emerging economies. Some 160,000 terminals are in use, and their numbers are growing by 17,000 to 25,000 a year, according to Price Waterhouse.

The characteristics of satellites vary with the distance from earth. Satellites cover more territory on earth as they move farther from it, but the transmission time increases, too. That causes a longer delay between broadcast and reception. It also takes more power to transmit a signal to a satellite that is farther from earth.

Geostationary satellites, which hover over a fixed point 22,300 miles above earth, are the farthest from earth. They have been a part of the telecommunications, broadcasting, weather forecasting, and surveillance businesses for four decades. They provide an essential backbone of the long-distance network, but they have only limited use for wireless phones. GEO satellite phones, which are as big as briefcases, cost as much as $25,000. The usage charges range up to $10 a minute.

Low-earth orbit satellites are spawning a new communications business. They are cheaper and less prone to delay than GEO satellites, making them a better choice for small portable phones or multimedia data services. Two examples: Iridium, owned by Motorola and 16 other investors, plans a $5 billion, 66-satellite voice and data network for late 1998. Teledesic, a joint venture of Craig McCaw and Bill Gates, plans a $9 billion, 840-satellite data network for 2002.

C-band satellites have been used to transmit television signals for years, and their large antennas are a familiar fixture on the rural landscape. But this market is shrinking as Direct Broadcast Satellite (DBS) becomes more popular. Digital DBS broadcasts, received with smaller antennas, are gaining popularity as an alternative to cable television. The big drawbacks so far are relatively high equipment costs and a lack of local programming. Both problems will be resolved over time, it appears. The major DBS carriers are DirectTv, run by GM's Hughes Electronics unit with an investment from AT&T; PrimeStar, owned by five big cable companies; and the result of the merger of Rupert Murdoch's and MCI's AskyB service with Echostar.

Raising Capital

Start-up companies hungry for cash often turn to the country's venture-capital community, a closely knit network of private investors who fund worthy young companies that are unable to issue stock or bonds. Venture capitalists have helped launch some of the best-known companies, from AT&T to Netscape.

The example of Vertical Networks shows what it takes to get the attention of venture capitalists. The company started with a powerful idea, something that everyone in the world—or at least a good percentage of the population—will find exciting and meaningful. Vertical Networks is still in its infancy, so the company won't discuss exactly what it is trying to create. Suffice to say, the company is constructing next-generation telecommunications networks that combine voice and data on a single high-speed line.

Vertical started with an experienced team, including Scott Picket, a National Semiconductor veteran who helped develop PCMCIA technology, those plug-in slots that allow people to instantly attach credit-card size modems, memory devices, and other devices to just about every laptop computer. The team also included Reed Henry, a Stanford MBA who participated in several corporate turnarounds.

They wrote a business plan and went to the top venture-capital firms in the world, asking for millions of dollars. They got it.

"How do you know?" asks Kevin Compton, the Kleiner Perkins Caufield & Byers partner responsible for funding Vertical. "More often than not, it's obvious. The great teams and great ideas just shine through." Kleiner Perkins is the same firm in Menlo Park, California, that funded Netscape, Marimba, Compaq Computer, and Sun Microsystems. Kleiner Perkins receives about 3,000 proposals a year. It shares its money—and its ideas, influence, connections, and support—with fewer than 20 of them.

"There are tremendous barriers to entry," admits Matthew Howard, who left Cisco to take a marketing job with Vertical. "It's very hard for a person without a name to raise cash and attract a good group of people."

Raising capital is always going to be a big challenge, but there are alternatives to the elite venture-capital firms such as Kleiner Perkins. There are private investors, corporations, friends and family, personal savings, and, for those moments when your back is hard against the wall, credit cards.

Kleiner Perkins keeps a tight rein on its purse, but it's more generous with advice. Two issues make or break a request for funding: the idea and the team. It's not the technology. Kleiner Perkins wants to know if the start-up venture at its doorstep is proposing something that people will actually want to go out and buy. Will the idea generate scale, and make something big happen? The ideas that are capable of stirring people are easily explained. They lend themselves to what Compton calls the "elevator pitch." That is, they can be explained between the first floor and the fourth. When Compton asks you to explain your idea, do not begin by stammering, "Well, it's really complicated."

A strong team must bring more than experience to the

venture. The leaders should be the sort of people who will draw other great people into the organization. Others should be eager to join the company just for the opportunity to work with them. They must also have proven ability to execute good ideas.

Venture-Capital Firms

Kleiner Perkins is one of about 300 venture-capital firms across the country that finance companies at the developmental stage, generally in exchange for a substantial stake in the business. They make about $3 billion worth of investments a year. Several dozen of these firms specialize in telecommunications and related fields. Raising venture capital is a rigorous process that will consume three-fourths of your time over a three-month period, advises Todd Degras, a partner at Battery Ventures L.P. in Boston, which specializes in funding communications.

"We want to know everything about your business," Degras says. Battery evaluates a company's business plan, paying close attention to marketing, technology, potential legal conflicts, and accounting practices. It wants to make sure, for example, that a young company hasn't prematurely reported revenues that have yet to materialize.

A start-up company that succeeds in attracting venture capital generally receives funds in three stages, or rounds. It's possible to raise all the money at once, although Degras advises against it. The initial round, known as seed funding, often comes from the entrepreneur or from a private investor known as an "angel," who will typically invest $500,000 to $1 million to design a prototype of a new product or otherwise prove that the company's concept can be executed.

The next step is called first-round financing. This is often the first point at which a venture capital firm such as Battery or Kleiner Perkins enters the process, taking over for the angel who funded the seed round. At this stage, the business plan and the technical designs have been completed, but commercial operation is about a year away. A substantial amount of money, anywhere from $2 million to $8 million, is needed to bring the business plan to life.

Round two begins when the new product is ready to ship or the company is otherwise ready to begin commercial operation. Yet more money—$5 million to $10 million—is needed to expand distribution channels and marketing campaigns.

A fourth step, known as the "mezzanine round," has traditionally been used as a bridge to a public offering, helping the company grow enough to attract the attention of the capital markets. The rules have changed in recent years, though. The demand among investors for new stock offerings is so high that many telecommunications companies are often able to skip the mezzanine round and proceed directly to the stock and bond markets.

Investment Banks

Once upon a time, companies had to show a profit and generate annual revenues of $20 million to $30 million before an investment bank would agree to issue its stock. That's no longer the case. There are many well-known examples of companies such as Netscape, or ones that have gone public merely on the strength of a powerful idea, turning the company's founders into millionaires or billionaires overnight. The stock often continues to rise even though the company may be months or years away from reporting revenues, let alone profits. The lure of participating in the growth of the next Microsoft or the next Intel is enough to keep many investors on-board.

An investment bank will often fund a company just before it goes public, when much of the risk has dissipated and there is a clear need to raise a lot of money, such as $10 million or more.

The fund-raising process usually begins with a meeting in which the company arrives armed with its business plan and a computer presentation arguing its merits. The business plan should address the basic issues of sales and marketing plans, products, staff, and financial projections. The presentation should honestly address the threat of competition. Degras says entrepreneurs are often weakest when it comes to assessing this risk. "If someone comes in and tells me they have no competition, they are either stupid or lying, or they haven't done their homework," he says. "If your market is worth going into, you will have competition."

You must have a credible plan for beating the competition: a solid team of managers and a competitive advantage, such as a patented technology or a head start in the market. It helps to pick a business where the barriers to entry are high enough to discourage a flood of other people from joining the fray. If your technological breakthrough can be duplicated or exceeded by a couple of college students in a dorm room—and many of them can be—you may have a problem.

If you do secure venture capital, you can expect to give up about half of your company in return. And if you take the company public, you can expect to give up about half your remaining stake to employees, leaving you with about 25 percent ownership. With that in mind, Degras says, it's crucial not to give away too much of the company in the early, or seed round, of financing. You will need to keep something to trade for money further along the way.

Corporate Investors

It's also possible to turn to established corporations, such as Microsoft and Intel, for funding. Intel alone has funded some 60 smaller companies. Degras advises entrepreneurs to avoid taking money from big corporations too early in the game. A company such as Intel or Microsoft, loaded with cash, will often nurture a small company for strategic reasons. It isn't making a financial investment, so much as nurturing a promising technology that it may need for its own business, or keeping some control over a potential competitor. It might be willing to pay more for a stake in the company than would a venture capitalist. That can be tempting for a company raising seed money, but it might drive the valuation of your company too high to raise money from a venture capitalist in succeeding rounds.

Sometimes the power of a big corporate investor is necessary, though. "If it's a big play like @home, then you probably need big partners like utilities or cable partners or whatever," says Compton of Kleiner Perkins.

CellularVision is a good example. The company developed a new technology known as Local Multipoint Distribution System (LMDS), which uses microwaves to create a two-way wireless system that is supposed to have the capacity of fiber-optic cable. It is designed to send and receive phone calls, data transmission, and television at high speed. Inventor Bernie Bossard, a veteran of the Patriot missile project, couldn't obtain venture capital because he didn't yet have a patent on the technology, which controls the tendency of microwave transmissions to break up in bad weather. In 1986, a sympathetic banker steered him toward the Hovnanian homebuilding empire in New Jersey, which was branching into the cable TV business. The partnership worked.

Bossard teamed up with Shant Hovnanian to create CellularVision USA, which is operating in New York. They are also licensing the technology to other companies in the United States and abroad, where governments are licensing more regional systems. The company, which hopes to construct a mass-market alternative to both phone and cable companies and Internet service providers, probably couldn't have achieved its scale or survived a long developmental period without big corporate backers. Bell Atlantic and J.P. Morgan bought 4 percent stakes, and Philips Electronics bought a 2 percent stake in the company.

Courting Private Investors

Another option, often attractive to medium-size companies, is to court private individual investors. That's what Richard

Keenan and Troy Dodson did when they launched Cashel Communications of Vancouver, Washington, in November 1993. They had worked for a prepaid phone provider called Bottom Line Communications. Keenan said he also helped the company raise funds for a spinoff called Talk and Toss, both of which were acquired by WorldCom in 1996. Keenan had also worked for MCI, and Dodson had worked for MCI and AT&T. They wanted to own a company, so they decided to provide telecommunications technology for companies overseas, drawing on international ties that went back to their days at AT&T and MCI. They turned to the same private investors they had courted for Talk and Toss, raising $1.5 million from 13 people.

Bootstrapping at the Outset

Most entrepreneurs will have to resort to the time-honored tradition of bootstrapping—scrapping together funds from savings and credit cards until their business starts generating cash. "On Day One I built it with cash," says Denis Raue, president and founder of Telegration, an agent, distributor, and reseller based in Troy, Michigan. He started out by telling his customers that he could save them a certain amount of money each month. When the savings materialized, they paid him two months' worth of savings. It was a successful formula, and the business now generates $15 million a year and has 67 full-time and part-time employees. Eventually, the business generated enough cash to support itself. But in the meantime: "You run up credit cards, you tell your wife you are going to work 80 hours a week for ten years, after which you are going to have a pretty good life."

Additional information:

The National Venture Capital Association represents about 200 firms that invest in young companies. The group is based at 1655 North Fort Myer Drive, Suite 700, Arlington, VA 22209. The telephone number is (703) 351-5269;

the fax number is (703) 351-5268 or (703) 525-8841. The group publishes a directory of its membership. Here is a selected list of venture-capital firms that have made significant investments in communications companies:

Accel Partners
One Palmer Square
Princeton, NJ 08542
(609) 683-4500
http://www.accel.com

Battery Ventures L.P.
200 Portland Street
Boston, MA 02114
(617) 367-1011

Greylock Management Corp.
One Federal Street, 26th floor
Boston, MA 02110
(617) 423-5525

Hancock Venture Partners
One Financial Center, 44th Floor
Boston, MA 02111
(617) 348-3707

Kleiner Perkins Caufield & Byers
2750 Sand Hill Road
Menlo Park, CA 94025
(415) 233-2750

Menlo Ventures
3000 Sand Hill Road
Building 4, Suite 100
Menlo Park, CA 94025
(415) 854-8540

Regulation & Taxation

The huge changes in the telecommunications laws should not be confused with deregulation. True, many fundamental restrictions on local, long-distance, and wireless telephony and TV markets have been dropped or eased, and businesses maneuver in those markets with greater freedom than ever before. Having said that, telecommunications remains among the most tightly regulated markets in the country. Layers of federal, state, and even municipal regulation will make demands on the entrepreneur at every turn; bureaucracy, paperwork, fees, and taxes abound. Patience and resolve will help you wend your way through the labyrinth of regulation.

And you will need money as well. According to Todd Lowe, president of Visiology, a regulatory consulting group, a nationwide reseller can spend $50,000 or more just to get started. The bills can rise to several hundred thousand dollars after lawyers fees and other expenses are included for nationwide approval. A consultant will typically charge $1,500 to $2,000 to prepare a long-distance rate plan and present it for approval. An application to offer local service in a single state can run an additional $3,000. A simple long-distance rate application, known as a tariff, can be prepared in a few days. But local tariffs are much longer and more complex.

The maze begins at the national level with the FCC, which has a say in long-distance, local, wireless, broadcasting, and the Internet. It is impossible to avoid. The agency imposes fewer demands on long-distance companies and resellers than it does on big, established local phone companies. It's up to the FCC, for example, to determine when the regional Bell phone companies have opened up their local markets to competition and are entitled to enter the long-distance market. The FCC only requires long-distance companies to inform the agency that they have entered the market, and to announce the services they provide and what they charge for domestic and international long-distance calls. It doesn't regulate those prices. It has determined that the market is now sufficiently competitive to keep rates in check. FCC fees begin at $1,345. The approval for interstate service can be received in a day. The approval for international service can take 50 days.

However, the maze explodes in complexity at the state level. "Switchless" resellers of long-distance service—those who don't own, operate, or lease any telecommunications networks of their own—will encounter one of four levels of regulation from public utility commissions across the country. These state regulators often demand that you file a tariff, a long document that explains your rates, terms, and conditions of service. They may reserve the right to approve or deny your rates, maintaining a prerogative that the FCC has long since abandoned. And that is just for starters.

State Regulation of Switchless Long-Distance Resellers

Deregulation

At the simplest level, a handful of states have decided not to regulate switchless long-distance resellers at all. These states include Colorado, Iowa, Michigan, New Jersey, Ohio, Utah, and Virginia.

Registration

Idaho, Kansas, Kentucky, Louisiana, Rhode Island, Texas, Washington, and Wyoming require a simple registration. You can do this through the mail, but the process generally takes one to three months. Some states charge up to several hundred dollars in one-time fees as well.

Registration simply informs the state's public utility commission that you will be reselling long-distance phone service within its borders. You may also have to file a copy of your rates and terms of service. You don't need the commission's approval, and it can't reject your registration.

Certification

About half the states require long-distance resellers to apply through the mail for permission to operate within their borders. The utility commissions in these states do have authority to reject your application, and the majority of them will make sure your rates and terms of service, known as a tariff, conform to their specifications. The process can take one to six months or more, and the one-time fees range from nothing to a few hundred dollars. You will have to file regular reports with utility commissions on an annual, quarterly, or monthly basis, keeping them up to date on your services and prices.

Certification with hearing

Alabama, Connecticut, Illinois, Maine, Missouri, Nebraska, and South Carolina require long-distance resellers to participate in a certification hearing. In some cases, the hearing can be waived or conducted over the telephone as long as the application isn't contested. Some of these states also require the applicant to bring a lawyer. The approval process usually takes one to six months, and one-time fees range from nothing to $1,000 in the case of Connecticut.

A note on switched resellers: The rules for resellers that incorporate their own telephone switches or transmission lines into their service are often more demanding than the rules for switchless resellers. In Colorado, for example, switchless resellers generally don't have to apply for certification, but switched resellers do. Winning certification across the country can take at least half a year and cost thousands of dollars in expenses for lawyers and travel. And the process continues after you win your initial certification. As a reseller, you will often be required to update utility commissions across the state every time you change your rates or services. As complicated as this sounds, certification with the public utilities commission is only the first hurdle in some states. Several layers of additional regulation often exist.

Certification of foreign corporation

About 30 states will require you to register with the secretary of state as a *foreign corporation*, unless you happen to be incorporated in that state. In Illinois, for example, resellers must register with the secretary of state unless they are based in Illinois. There are annual fees for this certification.

Registered agent

Nearly half the states will also require you to have a registered agent within their borders—that is, someone who is based in the state and will answer the state's call if your company runs into trouble. There is an annual fee for this service, too.

Every name that your business uses must be filed separately with the secretary of state. It makes sense to pick one corporate name that you can live with and stick to it. Don't register as "ABC Telco," on the assumption that you can pick a "real" name later. You will just increase the amount of your annual fees.

Legal notices

Many states also require long-distance resellers to publish small newspaper advertisements, known as *legal ads*, announcing that they have entered the market. This can be a considerable expense. In West Virginia, resellers have been required to publish as many as 19 legal ads. Other states may require you to send a letter to each of your competitors, letting them know you have arrived. In California, some companies have been required to send out 350 such announcements at a total cost of $15,000.

If these requirements sound complicated, remember this: They apply only to long-distance resellers. If you want to resell local or wireless phone service, a different set of rules apply. These areas are growing quickly as regulations change and more companies rush into the market. But they are so new that the rules governing these enterprises are still being written.

Wireless Companies and State Regulation

The FCC says states don't have jurisdiction over wireless phone service, but five state governments—California, Louisiana, New York, Vermont, and West Virginia—disagree and have imposed some restrictions on wireless companies. Their demands vary. At one end of the spectrum, California instructs wireless companies to fill out a relatively simple registration form. At the other end of the spectrum, Vermont asserts the right to approve or deny a complete tariff, including the rates, terms, and conditions or service.

Prepaid Calling Cards

A number of states—including Minnesota, Delaware, Washington, Nevada, South Carolina, and Louisiana— require companies to post large bonds in exchange for the right to offer prepaid phone services. The bonds range from $3,000 to $50,000, warns Andrew Isar, of Harbor Consulting.

Local Companies

The states have regulated local telephone service since the early days of the 20th century. They have developed huge, powerful commissions to oversee even bigger, more powerful local phone monopolies. The states began to dismantle the local phone monopolies a few years ago, paving the way for the sort of competition that exists in the long-distance market. Most state utility commissions have adopted rules that allow competitors into their local markets. Competition is still in the early stages of development, although it could explode in the near future. So far, most competitors are targeting high-spending businesses instead of consumers.

If you want to resell local phone service, be prepared to contend with powerful state bureaucracies. "It's a difficult process, three to five times more expensive and time-consuming than meeting the regulatory requirements for long-distance resellers," says Todd Lowe, of Visiology. The tariffs he has prepared for companies that want to resell local phone service have run 400 to 500 pages in length. A few states have one certification or registration process for resale of local and long-distance service, but about two-thirds of the states require a separate application. In Oregon, for example, long-distance resellers can enter the local market after they file a relatively simple modification to their certification, Lowe says. But Massachusetts requires local resellers to file a separate tariff, even if they are already certified to provide long-distance service.

Many states force small resellers to abide by rules that were established for large Bell telephone companies. In Arkansas, for example, resellers can't demand payment from a customer until 22 days after a bill is rendered. "You would think I could go in and offer a lower rate and say I want a quicker payment in return, but I can't," Lowe says.

Many states, particularly in the Northeast, force resellers to provide phone service to just about anyone that demands it, regardless of their credit history. Local phone companies had to abide by many rules in exchange for their monopolies over the market. They had to keep rates low and couldn't cut off a customer's service at will. In some states, a phone customer is considered creditworthy as long as they can demonstrate that the local power company hasn't shut off service in the last year, or sent them more than two termination notices.

Many utility commissions forbid local phone companies from demanding deposits from customers with poor credit records, although they can't prevent you from demanding a deposit for long-distance service.

The price of compliance is high, but the price of noncompliance is higher still. State utility commissions have no sympathy for companies that flout their rules, and they are making it difficult for companies to avoid them. The Florida utility commission now prohibits a carrier from providing long-distance service to an uncertified reseller, essentially making the established local phone company a deputy.

After considering the time, effort, and risks of certification, you may decide to make life easier by hiring a regulatory attorney or a consulting firm to help you work your way through the maze. The fees for a nationwide applicant can run several hundred thousand dollars. In exchange, the attorney or consultant will fill out the forms and shepherd them through the regulatory process. While costly, this service will allow you, the entrepreneur, to focus on the other aspects of getting your business started. In the end, though, many telecommunications companies assign one or more people on the inside to manage their regulatory affairs.

"I hired a regulatory attorney," says Doug Furbush, president of Trans National Communications, a long-distance reseller based in Boston. "Using him, and one person internally, it took three years to get regulatory approval in all 50 states." It cost the firm $200,000.

Some firms specialize in every aspect of certification—from public utility certification, to registering as a foreign corporation with the secretary of state, to finding registered agents to represent your company. A consulting firm will often charge $30,000 a year to maintain registered agents across the country. They maintain a contact in every state, or are affiliated with another group that does.

One general recommendation is to request that the commission exempt the reseller from regulation. According to Lowe, that reduces the initial certification costs and the long-term costs associated with regulation.

Tips on filing an application

Make sure you have all your financial statements well organized, says Andrew Isar, of Harbor Consulting. The documents typically required include income statements, balance sheets, guarantees of financing, anything that will enhance the credibility of your financial representation. Pay careful attention to how you price your services. Regulators are geared toward protecting consumers in their states, and they won't look kindly upon companies that gouge their constituents.

Regulatory consultants

Visiology Inc.
Todd Lowe, President
16061 Carmel Bay Drive
Northport, AL 35476
(205) 331-1701
Specializes in winning approval from state public utility authorities

Harbor Consulting
P.O. Box 2461
5210 Reid Drive
Gig Harbor, WA 98335
(206) 265-3910

Unisearch
101 Capital Way
Olympia, WA 98501
(800) 722-0708
Specializes in registering your company as a foreign corporation and establishing registered agents

Beware of Slamming

Regulators place a lot of demands on law-abiding companies that play by the rules. Can you imagine how they treat companies that don't?

The easiest way to get in trouble is to switch a customer to your service without obtaining the customer's permission. The problem is common enough to have earned its own nickname—slamming.

Anyone who provides phone service to the public must make sure that they are authorized to change a subscriber's long-distance or local phone service. Some companies and rogue telemarketing agents have been known to flout the law. The FCC extracts a high price when it catches up to them—$40,000 for a single "egregious" violation.

Even a well-intentioned company can run afoul of the slamming laws. A customer can run up high charges, refuse to pay the bill, and then accuse you of switching his or her service without permission. Then it's up to your company to defend itself before the regulators.

Many violations fall somewhere between such egregious violations on the part of customer or service provider. Take a look at how changes in service are processed, and you'll understand why it's easy to make a mistake. Let's say that a telemarketer makes a successful pitch, and the customer, at line 555-555-1234, agrees to switch long-distance companies. As the telemarketer takes the order, he transposes two digits while typing the order at his computer terminal. Suddenly, the customer at line 555-555-1243 has been slammed.

A few safeguards can protect you against that sort of error. You should always have two people type the change into your computer system. If one of them makes a mistake, the discrepancy will prevent the incorrect order from going through. And you can go a step further and hire an independent consultant to verify the changes. These companies will call the customer and make sure that the change in service is correct and has been authorized. In California, resellers are required to hire a third party to verify each change in long-distance carrier.

Slamming can cost a company a lot of money and damage its reputation quickly. The FCC maintains a slamming scorecard that is available to the public on the World Wide Web.

Third-Party Verifiers

Sierra Technologies
8753 Broadway, Suite H
La Mesa, CA 91941
(619) 462-4480

Third Party Verification Inc.
5601 East Slauson Avenue, Suite 211
Commerce, CA 90040
(800) 615-5000

Taxes: the Telecom Nightmare

Long-distance companies pay a levy to the federal government and nearly all states nationwide. Thousands of counties and municipalities tax the industry, too. Your business may even have to pay taxes in villages that are too small to qualify as fully independent towns. The very largest long-distance carriers, which have customers in pretty much every town across the country, pay taxes to 1,500 to 3,000 jurisdictions. And those bills are often due monthly.

Some states, such as Alabama, have separate taxes for wireless phone companies. And as the states open their local phone markets to competition, every layer of government will charge its own admission price.

The average telecommunications company spends about 7.5 percent of its revenue on taxes, says Gary Rhodus, president of Atlantax, an Atlanta consulting group that specializes in telecommunications taxation. In Florida, where nearly every town imposes a levy of its own, a telecommunications company can expect to spend about 20 cents on the dollar to pay taxes. In states such as Nevada, where only a federal excise tax applies, the rate is about 3 percent, says Rhodus, who spent 23 years in the Bell System and three years at BellSouth before he struck out on his own in 1991. Rhodus, who worked on tax issues stemming from the breakup of the Bell System in 1984, now advises about 100 telecommunications companies on tax issues.

The biggest carriers, serving nearly every town, village, and hamlet across the country, must file 1,500 to 3,000 tax returns a month. The second-tier carriers operate nationwide, but only in the sense that they do business in all 50 states. They don't necessarily operate in every local jurisdiction, instead focusing their attention on businesses in larger metropolitan markets. So they file fewer returns.

"Our experience is that any telecommunications company doing business nationally—the average resale company—probably files 250 tax returns a month," Rhodus says. The nature of those taxes is literally all over the map, in that it varies wildly from state to state. At the state level, 47 of the 50 states and the District of Columbia tax telecommunications services. The differences begin at the local level within those states.

In Florida, California, and Illinois, for example, just about every municipality has a utilities tax. In Colorado, a tradition of home rule allows towns that were chartered when Colorado was still a territory to levy their own taxes. But newer towns can't. In New York, telecommunications companies file only one tax return, but it includes numerous taxes for cities and towns across the state. That's why a company filing 250 tax returns is really paying taxes to 1,000 jurisdictions across the country.

Telecommunications companies will face a more difficult tax issue as they enter the local market, where monopolies are ending. They will have to worry about special classes of taxes, such as the current subscriber line charge that appears on local phone bills nationwide. Or they will have to worry about the so-called "franchise fee." These special taxes may be replaced by new taxes and fees, but they will exist in one form or another. Rhodus says a nationwide database for the current generation of fees doesn't even exist, since there hasn't been a nationwide local market before. Even when the Bell System was part of AT&T, the local operating companies operated with great independence within each state.

As the industry evolves, it's not exactly clear what constitutes a taxable service. Emergency 911 service, telephone relay services for the hearing impaired, and other service fees all raise questions about what should be taxed.

Rhodus says some smaller companies prefer to file their own taxes, especially in states such as Kansas, Colorado, and Nebraska, where only 20 or 30 returns are required. But most companies, at a minimum, have an outside accountant or consultant work with someone on their own staff.

Commerce Clearing House, a law book publisher in Chicago, sells telecom tax tables in book format for a few hundred dollars a year, and doesn't charge any initial fee for the service. But you have to enter the tax rates into your computers and check them for accuracy, and the cost of making a mistake can be huge.

Managing Growth

United Telecommunications, a local phone company that traced its roots to the late 19th century, seized the long-distance opportunity in the early 1980s. It was just a medium-sized carrier at the time, with networks in rural and suburban areas scattered across 19 states. Management had lofty ambitions, though, in the long-distance market. Its designs went far beyond the popular strategy of buying service from a bigger player and reselling it to the public at a competitive price. United's dream was to build a new nationwide network from scratch, using the latest long-distance technology: fiber-optic cables that transmitted information as flashes of light. It was much faster than the old method of sending voice over a copper wire, and United picked a natural name for its new service: Sprint.

Construction required billions in capital, but the company was certain it could handle the project. After all, it was run by William Esrey, a young banker who had spent ten years on Wall Street and financed many communications deals. The company built the network and signed up millions of customers, yet within four years it was in deep trouble. Debt was out of hand, and the company's billing system was overloaded by the unexpected demand for its service.

It's the classic example of how growth can be the kiss of death for even the most skilled and well-capitalized communications company. Sprint survived the crisis, of course. Today, it's the third largest long-distance carrier in the United States, and it still retains the old local business. The latest expansion projects include a nationwide digital wireless network and alliances with France Telecom and Deutsche Telekom. Yet Esrey candidly admits the company nearly crashed in the early stages because of a common problem. Communications companies must make their big investments *before* they sign up customers. They must grow as quickly as possible to recoup their start-up costs, but the quicker they grow, the deeper they sink in debt. "There is no way to avoid up-front losses," warns Esrey.

The Cash-Flow Challenge

The risk of failure in telecommunications is significant. About 17.5 percent of telecommunications resellers failed to produce a profit in 1996, although the figure was about 25 percent the year before. Consolidation has removed many marginal companies from the scene; others have simply gone out of business. Many of those problems revolve around the management of cash flow and growth.

"Cash flow is challenging. When you are in growth mode, you can have so much money in motion that you put yourself out of business," says Gene Chase, the owner of Pantel, a long-distance reseller with about 40,000 customers, mostly in the residential market. The inevitable early losses can be overcome—many companies, from Sprint to Pantel, have done it—but careful management of cash flow, expenses, and operations is crucial.

"If you are the world's greatest salesman, and that's it, set yourself up as an agent on commission. You will make more money and sleep better," says Todd Lowe, president of Visiology, a telecom consulting group. "This isn't a sales business. It's a management business. You don't get into it unless you know how to manage cash in the first place. Otherwise, you fail."

As a consultant for Allnet in Chicago during the early 1980s, Lowe helped get one of the long-distance industry's first resellers off the ground. He developed a business plan that set a blistering pace for the young company, which sought to double its revenues every quarter. As the company began commercial operation, Lowe was hired full-time to run information systems, and confronted the difficulties of bringing the plan to life. The company eventually merged with Frontier because it couldn't pull itself out of what Lowe calls the cash-flow trap.

A long-distance reseller—let's call it UltraCom—opens for business in February, selling $10,000 worth of service. In the process, it incurs a $7,000 bill with the carrier that supplies it with wholesale phone service.

UltraCom's $7,000 bill with its supplier must be paid in March; UltraCom customers won't pay their February phone bills until early April. There are several reasons for the delay: It takes time to determine how much customers owe, and it takes additional time to deliver the bills. Once they arrive, custom dictates that your customers are entitled to a grace period before their payments are due. So UltraCom enters its second month with a negative cash flow, and its problems are going to get worse before they get better. Similar traps exist in other lines of work, but it's exacerbated by the high growth rates in telecommunications.

The problem will get worse. UltraCom is growing quickly, and it sells an additional $20,000 worth of long-distance service during March. Those sales also incur a cost: an additional $14,000 bill with its supplier.

As April begins, UltraCom finally starts to receive the $10,000 in cash that it earned in February. The problem is that UltraCom has already logged $21,000 in bills with its underlying carrier, including $7,000 in February and

$14,000 in March. After just three months, this vibrant, quickly growing start-up venture has achieved a negative cash flow of $11,000. And it hasn't even paid its marketing costs, sales commissions, salaries, or rent.

This nightmare will eventually end. UltraCom will continue to increase revenues by $10,000 a month. Each month that increase in sales will represent a smaller percentage of its monthly revenue. Eventually, that percentage will fall below the margin of profit, and that is when UltraCom's cash flow will turn positive. It won't reach that crossroads automatically, though. The business must be carefully managed along the way, to minimize its cash-flow problems and keep expenses down.

Avoiding the Cash-Flow Trap

A telecommunications company can often achieve a positive cash flow in a year and a half, but it's more difficult than it was in the 1980s and early 1990s. Many companies in the long-distance industry once enjoyed cash-flow margins of 35 or 40 percent. But competition has driven margins down to 20 to 25 percent, or less. It takes more time and skill to build a strong company with a positive cash flow.

Entrepreneurs are a creative lot, and many of the best have a flair for keeping costs under control. David Walker, a commercial developer in Albuquerque, New Mexico, decided to branch into the long-distance resale business in 1988, just as it was starting to really boom. He ran the operation out of a building that he already owned, eliminating the need to pay rent. Then he took the ingenious step of limiting his first commercial offerings to toll-free business lines. "We sold discounts on 800 service. We called people on their 800 number so our phone bill was not very high," says Walker. When he received a 27 percent discount from his carrier, he passed a 20 percent discount along to his customers, and he kept the rest for himself. It was a modest start, but the business was in the black within six months, thanks to Walker's tight control on costs. The business, which now offers a full range of long-distance and Internet services, generates $15 million a year in revenue from small- and medium-size business accounts in New Mexico.

Chase, the owner of Pantel, found another way out of the cash-flow trap. He borrowed a technique from the retail industry and acquired the service of a factoring company. A factoring company lends money to businesses so they can purchase inventory. The borrower stocks his store (or in this case, his network) with product and sells it to the public. He repays the loan to the factoring company after his customers have paid their bills. The drawback is that factoring companies, like any bank, charge a fee.

Other resellers use prepaid calling cards to improve their cash flow. The beauty of the prepaid calling card business is that the customer pays you before you pay your supplier. Many people have made money by venturing into this niche. But even if you're trying to build a broader business, a prepaid calling-card division can provide some financial ballast.

Over the years, Lowe has developed a set of principles to help clients of his consulting firm survive the dangers of a high-growth communications company in the start-up phase. Perhaps the most important lesson is that growth for growth's sake leads to trouble. Grow quickly, but make sure the growth makes sense within the structure of your business plan. "Growth can be a narcotic," Lowe says. "You can lose sight of the real goal: to make money."

Here are some suggestions for keeping that goal in sight:

Make sure you establish a good relationship with your banker early in the start-up process: Present the bank with a conservative business plan as soon as possible, one that assumes a worst-case scenario. Resellers fail when their underlying carrier demands payment, and they run to a bank that isn't willing to lend them more money. It's important to borrow the money before you run into trouble. And borrow more than you think you will need.

Watch your receivables like a hawk: Your cash-flow problems will only get worse if your customers don't pay you on time. The average customer's bill needs to be paid within 40 days, and you can't let the stragglers go more than 60. There is little to be gained by canceling a customer's service. More than likely, the customer will simply find another carrier and you will have lost your leverage in the situation. Your chance of collecting a payment decreases as the bill becomes more and more overdue.

The pressure to keep your accounts current is growing. Back in 1983, when Lowe was working for Allnet, telecommunications companies could tolerate a default rate of up to 3 percent. Today, they must limit defaults to 1 percent. Profit margins have decreased, and telecom companies simply can't afford to write off any bad debt.

Even big companies such as AT&T are vulnerable to customer credit problems, especially when consumer or business bankruptcies are running high. AT&T's Universal credit card unit had a problem in late 1996 with business customers who weren't paying their bills on time. The problem lowered AT&T earnings in early 1997. The company's two-year plan to cut expenses by $2 billion in 1997 and 1998 makes credit quality a top priority. If bad debt can cause that much of a stir inside a $52 billion corporation that invented the telephone more than a century ago, imagine the havoc it can wreak inside a start-up venture.

One solution is to sell your bad debts to a collection agency or an investor. Some people specialize in making people pay up on bad debts, and it can be very profitable once they do. You can also turn to factoring, as Allnet did.

Keep expenses low: In the best of times, this discipline will help you make the most out of your business. In the worst of times, it will save you from collapse. Laura Scher, the chief executive of Working Assets, said the company faced a crisis in 1986. It was marketing credit cards in conjunction with State Street Bank in Boston. Working

Assets, a pioneer of affinity marketing that targeted politically active consumers with a liberal bent, agreed to sell 10,000 cards in a three-year period. All the cards were sold out between March and June 1986. The bank decided it didn't want to proceed with the deal, forcing Working Assets to halt a big part of its business. "We were very leanly managed; we probably had eight people," Scher recalls. "If we hadn't looked like that, if we had lots of people on staff, we would have gone out of business or had a big downsizing."

Many entrepreneurs have a knack for getting other people to work for them for free. RCN's David McCourt bought a television station in Grenada in the 1980s. He used an old Cuban embassy as a dormitory and brought in college students from the United States to run the station. The students worked without salary for the experience and the college credit. Classes of Grenadian students studied in the United States in a reciprocal arrangement. That allowed him to develop a new domestic student labor pool as well.

In the United States, multilevel marketers such as Excel have cut salaries using a system in which salespeople recruit new sales people and take a percentage of their recruits' profits. People make money only if they bring new and productive salespeople into the organization.

Keep your customers happy: This is one area where you should not skimp. You have to grow your customer-service organization. You can hire someone else to do it, but assume the task yourself as soon as possible.

It's actually easier to manage thousands of calls a day than it is to mange hundreds. The economy of scale improves. Smaller groups of sales agents tend to get overloaded with too many callers. That means customers who call during peak hours endure longer delays, and the last thing you want to do is put your customers on hold when they call customer service. It's worth the effort to sufficiently staff your service department, because the cost of servicing existing customers is lower than the cost of soliciting new ones.

Remember that everything will happen slower than you anticipate: It will take longer than expected to sign a contract with a carrier, sign up customers, and get paid. Leave yourself plenty of time for each step.

Write a business plan and stick to it: "This is not a plan you use once to raise money and then throw in a drawer," Lowe warns. "It should be a living document."

Know your limits: Lowe advises telecommunications companies to go national right away, but if you aren't extremely well-financed, that probably isn't the right plan. Smaller resellers are generally advised to start in one or two strategic markets. That will give you a chance to build a base of profitable operations to fund your expansion.

If you begin with a small, tight geographic area, you can probably get started with a few hundred thousand dollars. "You could do it with $100,000 if you start as a reseller, take it slow, and find a friendly banker. That would be enough to start a switchless resale business in one or two states," Lowe says.

Lowe advises similar caution when it comes to investing in equipment. It's more profitable to own your own switches, the network computers that connect one phone to another as a call is placed. The profit margins are higher if you don't have to lease the use of another company's switch. But the price of a very basic switch starts in raw form at $65,000 or $70,000. Bigger switches often cost millions. Don't let the strong rationale for owning your own equipment push you into serious debt trouble.

Esrey says one of Sprint's early mistakes was to let capital investments get out of hand, in the belief that these investments had to be made sooner or later anyway. Many businesses have started out with a few services and added on as they grew. After all, Sprint waited nearly 100 years to expand from local phone service to long-distance.

Leadership

Leaving the transmission lines and high-tech networks for others to build, Kenny Troutt designed his phenomenally successful long-distance company, Excel Communications, around another sort of network, a human one. The heart of the company is a carefully constructed network of salespeople drawn from other human networks of family and friends.

"Seventy-five percent of our success comes from our reps out there," Troutt says. His famous seven-level sales force has propelled the company's annual revenues from nothing to $1.4 billion in just eight years. The former Texas oilman with a populist politician's feel for the masses says the secret is "lots of huggin' and kissin' and kissin' and huggin'."

Excel is the biggest and most successful of the country's 1,000 long-distance resellers, and it didn't get that way by accident. It is a perfect example of how entrepreneurial companies reflect the personality of their founder and leader. In this case, the leader had global ambitions. "I needed to come up with a marketing plan that would enable me to mobilize masses of people able to take us worldwide and nationwide," Troutt says.

He developed a multilevel sales force similar to the door-to-door Amway troops. Excel buys long-distance service at wholesale rates from big carriers, such as WorldCom, and resells it in the residential market at a discount. But instead of hawking his wares in the mass media, Troutt designed a sales force that sells by word of mouth to friends, relatives, neighbors, and other acquaintances. Salespeople make money by recruiting more salespeople. They take a cut of the commissions earned by the people they bring into the system, as well as a cut of commissions earned by their recruits' recruits. Hence, the sales force is impelled to create an organization of great scope.

The reps earn more money and more recognition as they climb the rungs of the seven-step ladder, fulfilling what Troutt believes people really want. He promises them they can change their lives and earn as much money as they desire, so long as they are willing to pay the price. "What motivates people is money and recognition," he says. "In the beginning, it's money. Over time, it's recognition… After they are recognized, they will work harder to get recognized at a different level."

Unleashing Raw Ambition

Excel's structure is designed to unleash raw human ambition and apply the resulting energy to the growth of the business. And it does so with the efficiency of a finely tuned machine. After four years of middling, but respectable, growth, Excel was nowhere near fulfilling Troutt's ambitions. He decided that the answer was simply that the sales reps needed the opportunity to make more money. He announced the new commission plan at a company meeting in April 1993, sparking ten minutes of pandemonium and applause. That energy and enthusiasm showed up six months later in the company's revenues.

"We did $20 million the year before and it went to $32 million, $103 million, then $525 million, then $1.4 billion,"

Troutt says. One sales rep made $1.2 million in a single month. And Excel, which acquired competitor Vartec in 1997, is the sixth largest long-distance carrier in the United States. It expects to increase revenues to $4 billion or $5 billion within a few years.

In a network of people, Troutt stands at the center as leader and catalyst. Every entrepreneurial organization needs one: someone with a strong sense of where the organization is going, and the conviction to drive it forward despite uncertainty and risk. And the best leaders, like Troutt, also have an innate ability to harness the energy of other people in the group. For better or worse, this leader will stamp the organization with his or her vision, to apply an apt, though overused, word. That individualism distinguishes entrepreneurial companies from other enterprises, such as big corporations. Excel's character and success evolved directly from Troutt's global ambitions and his simple, lucid understanding of what he was after and how he could achieve it.

He started out with an unusually focused plan: "I needed to make a career change. Oil had dropped to $8 or $9 a barrel," he recalls. "I wanted to find something I could work the rest of my life at, something everybody used. Something simple. I was looking to take a product, build a customer base, and sell more products back to them. I was looking for something recession-proof. Looking for nationwide and worldwide growth and residual income. Put all these things together and what you get is the communications business. So I zeroed in on that. I did test studies and saw how easy it was. What I had to do was mobilize a sales force that could take me nationwide and worldwide."

There's a largeness of this vision, and it shaped the company. There are close to 1,000 telecommunications resellers in the United States, and Excel didn't become number one by accident. Most of his competitors had a vision something along these lines: "I can buy long-distance service at 12 cents a minute and sell it for 14 cents a minute, make a decent profit, and see where the business takes me," Troutt says. "Maybe I can retire early and enjoy life."

That's a perfectly serviceable goal and one that has launched the career of many a millionaire. But the really great businesses are usually created by entrepreneurs with a grandiose, world-conquering, and unconventional view of life. Few people can imagine themselves or their business on that scale and maintain the discipline to achieve that growth without self-destructing. Troutt never imagined himself as another AT&T or MCI, with thousands of miles of his own fiber in the ground. He kept careful control over acquisitions, expansion plans, and expenses. Sure, he was grandiose, but he was also realistic.

Troutt also exhibited another crucial characteristic of the great entrepreneur: the willingness to confront uncertainty and risk. Even now, Troutt is planning a nationwide expansion into the local phone business. And he's going to do it as a reseller, which many people regard as the worst possible strategy in a generally untenable business. Yet Troutt is willing to enter the market on the assumption that conditions will improve. He stands to lose on a large scale if he's wrong. But if he's right, he'll be one of a handful of people poised to capitalize on more favorable rules for newcomers. He's assuming a mantle of leadership by joining the first wave of new entrants in the residential local market.

"I think the local phone business is probably going to be our most powerful product," he says. "I'm not saying it's a good product today. But… somebody is going to have to jump in the water and prove that it's not over everybody's head."

No Leader is Immortal

The close identification of entrepreneurs to their companies creates a special hazard. What happens when the leader can't lead anymore—when illness, death, or old age intrude, or when the organization outgrows the founder's ability to run it? Entrepreneurs often fail to groom successors, and the repercussions can be disastrous.

"CEO pay should be one-third based on developing a succession plan," says Dennis Carey, vice chairman of Spencer Stuart USA, a top executive-recruiting firm that helped place Lou Gerstner at IBM. The third largest recruiting firm in the country, Spencer Stuart has handled two recent executive searches for AT&T. It was one of the firms that lured John Walter from printer R.R. Donnelly & Sons in November 1996. He became president of AT&T on the promise that he would succeed Bob Allen as chairman and chief executive in 1998. The board then developed reservations about the succession plan, and Walter resigned just nine months later. AT&T rehired Spencer Stuart to help fill the vacancy created by Walter's departure. Carey helped lure Hughes Electronics CEO C. Michael Armstrong to AT&T as chairman and CEO. AT&T's shares have since rallied to an all-time record.

Carey says companies large and small, old and new, must develop "next of kin" executives—people who will take over when the chief leaves. "They should be introduced to media outlets and Wall Street," says Carey. "They should be encouraged to join other boards of directors so they learn the difference between management and governance." They should include these next-generation CEOs in an office of the chairman, where they will be exposed to the business plans and strategies at the top of the company. And the human drama and competition should be limited by creating a predictable succession process. Once the issue of succession is settled, the political problems of dueling executives can be more easily contained.

The qualities that make good business leaders revolve around teamwork these days, especially in smaller companies where staff is limited in size. "The smaller the organization, the more utility infielders are required," Carey says. "By definition, you need people who are horizontally driven as opposed to vertically driven. You see a lot of cases in which the CFO is also the chief legal counsel, the controller, and the auditor, while also operating other parts of the business. It's vital you get people who are more broadly gauged, less hung-up over title and functional positions, and much more team-oriented. If you are not a team player in a small organization, you can do a lot of damage pretty quickly. Even most of these people have high ego needs, as most people do, but they tend to be flexible and adaptable. Those who aren't fail very quickly."

Information Technology and the Customer

Information technology (IT) is at the heart of the new tele communications business. Mining market statistics to learn about customers, developing and rapidly deploying new products to meet their needs, maintaining a fail-safe network, offering a full range of services—these are the definitive traits of a telecom company in the age of competition and digital networks. They all rely on a strong technological foundation. Many an entrepreneur has concluded that information technology is simply the critical factor in a successful communications venture. "Information in this game is your biggest asset," says Gene Chase, a computer programmer who built a long-distance company around a billing system of his design.

Information technology is closely linked to the development of durable relationships with customers, which is at the cutting edge of telecom strategy today. Of all the reasons that companies use to justify their IT investments—such as improving timeliness or reducing costs—the primary reason is to improve customer service, *Information*

Week reports. And the second most important reason is to target new customers, it found in a 1997 survey of 500 big companies that rely heavily on information technology. *Winning new customers is three times more expensive than retaining an existing customer*, so companies work hard to keep the ones they already have. Customers are less likely to switch when they depend on a company for a broad range of reliable services. A carrier needs the best billing systems, market analysis, and the network operating systems to deliver those services.

The computer systems that telecom companies relied on for decades weren't designed to meet those needs, and they are being rapidly replaced. Big carriers for years relied on mainframe computers that ran proprietary programs. They weren't designed to communicate with other systems. That puts them squarely at odds with three important trends: (1) the relentless mergers and acquisitions forcing companies to merge their databases, (2) the need for long-distance and local carriers to integrate their databases as they expand into new markets, and (3) the need to communicate with other carriers in the booming wholesale market. Finally, these companies must upgrade their networks to take advantage of the latest software, which doesn't conform to their outmoded, private standards.

Giant carriers are spending billions to overhaul their proprietary systems and develop flexible new information systems that conform to the Internet and other industry standards. Telecom companies spend more than twice as much on information technology as other industries—about 6 percent—compared to a cross-industry average of 2.9 percent, *Information Week* says. AT&T, for example, is spending billions on a new billing and information system called AT&T Render and Collect. Bell Atlantic has spent $600 million over the last five years to develop a new billing and information system called Express Track. It will unite antiquated databases that were built for separate operating units that never had to exchange information before.

And GTE is overhauling the software that runs its network with the GTE Integrated Systems Plan, a three-year project scheduled for completion in 2000. It's building a new network platform for voice, video, and data; an Internet-based internal information system; and a new framework for developing services.

Newcomers must be competitive with these giants, and they arrive with both an advantage and a disadvantage. They aren't burdened with incompatible systems based on obsolete technology. They don't need to waste time and money rebuilding old systems. They can start fresh with software that performs better and costs less. Yet big companies have an easier time financing these projects, which often cost millions of dollars. Many small companies can't afford their own systems. But even small carriers that resell other companies' service should be familiar with trends in information technology. They must look for partners that can supply them with state-of-the-art information technology.

These systems can be divided into two groups: those that manage the network and those that manage relationships with the customer.

Managing the Network

Network management has four components, says analyst Jeffrey Cotrupe, of Northern Business Information:

* Monitor the network to measure traffic and identify and correct faults.

* Take orders from customers.

* Connect with other networks operated by other carriers.

* Create, install, and operate new features such as Caller ID.

Telecommunications companies have an increasing number of choices as they meet these needs. The creation of these operations support systems (OSS) is a $12 billion-a-year industry, Cotrupe says. Companies can spend tens of millions of dollars to built a system from scratch, or they can hire another company to manage their network for them.

Many middle- to large-size carriers build their own systems, as they have done for decades. But today these systems are designed around a new multimedia industry standard known as Telecom Management Network (TMN). A new generation of software companies in Silicon Valley is sprouting up around the telecom industry. These companies develop software programs that are used to create operations support systems for telecom companies, using the TMN standard.

Bell Canada turned to Objective Systems Integrators (OSI) in 1993 when it needed a new operations support system for its local and long-distance networks, which are mostly in Ontario and Quebec. OSI executive Chris Simon was associate director of corporate engineering for Bell Canada at the time. The company wanted to develop a sophisticated new service for Pizza Hut, but its operations support systems weren't up to the task. Pizza Hut was exploring the idea of developing a single toll-free number that would serve large swaths of territory across North America. The idea was still being tested in late 1997, as Pepsi spun off Pizza Hut, KFC, and Taco Bell as Tricon Global Restaurants Inc. Tricon declined to discuss the project.

The idea is that callers across parts of the United States and Canada will be able to call a single toll-free phone number that would instantly connect them to the closest Pizza Hut restaurant. The concept breaks the old model of associating a phone number with a single place, by allowing many restaurants across the continent to use the same phone number. The network analyzes the incoming number, figures out where it's coming from, and switches it. The service could be developed using a Bellcore system known as Advanced Intelligent Network (AIN), widely deployed by Bell Canada and other major carriers. AIN is a system of computers within the network that allows phone companies to quickly create new services without having their switch manufacturers reprogram all their switches. It speeds up deployment of new services and puts the process in the control of the carrier, not the switch maker.

Bell Canada wanted to help Pizza Hut develop the service. It needed to keep track of all the new phone numbers —up to 50,000 a day—that changed in its territory. Then it related those phone numbers to ZIP codes. Next, the system needed to relate the ZIP code to a region in Pizza Hut's own corporate map. And finally, it had to link the call to a specific store.

Bell Canada's former operations system couldn't manage the enormous amount of data that the service needed to keep functioning. So the carrier asked OSI to help it develop a new one, says Simon, who views the ongoing project as an example of the crucial role that information technology plays in developing and deploying progressive new telecommunications services.

"My view is that operating support systems (OSS) are going to be how carriers differentiate themselves and how they become successful," he says. "Everybody can buy the network. If everyone has access to the same switches and AIN boxes, how are you going to win? By getting your services to market faster, and a lot depends on OSS."

OSI's Net Expert conforms to the Telecom Management Network standard, which operates at four levels:

- Element management, monitoring individual pieces of equipment, such as switches.

- Network management, monitoring individual pieces of equipment linked together in the network.

- Service management, monitoring the applications that ride the network; deploys and manages features such as call forwarding and caller ID.

- Business management, which analyzes whether the company has deployed enough equipment to meet its needs.

"These layers eat up a tremendous amount of staff in traditional regional Bell operating companies, if they are not mechanized," Simon says. Older carriers hire thousands of workers to enter and re-enter data into the system by hand every time a new customer requests service. That wastes time and money and increases the chance of error. He says new operations support systems reduce that busy work: "A new competitive local exchange carrier will put in the right system and reduce staff needed for provisioning, fault management, and correction."

OSI provides the underpinnings for the rapid development of an operations support system in six to nine months, at a cost of several hundred thousand dollars to more than $10 million, according to Simon, OSI's vice president of service provider solutions. The company, which has about 500 employees and revenues of about $50 million a year, is equipped to integrate old-fashioned databases into newer software systems. It can accommodate networks that carry voice, video, or other types of data. Customers include regional Bell companies, competitive local exchange carriers, wireless carriers, cable TV companies, and even banking networks of automatic teller machines.

Carriers don't need to invest in an entire operations support system all at once. Many begin with a billing and customer-care system. The next step often depends on how many switches the carrier has deployed. If the network has limited capacity, it might invest in a performance-monitoring system, which monitors the flow of traffic and looks for congestion. If the network has plenty of switches and the carrier is confident that the network is performing well, it might invest in a fault-detection system. It will search for errors in the system instead of monitoring traffic. A fraud-management system is often added along the way.

Operating support systems aren't used to create new calling features, but they are used to deploy them. The ability to quickly fill a new order for service is crucial. Many small businesses are still complaining about the many months their local phone company needed to install higher-speed ISDN phone lines. It often took months. Those delays erode the goodwill of the customer and cut into profit margins. "The first carrier to deploy an enhanced service can charge more for it until other people implement it," says Bruce Brown, CEO of Vertel, an OSS maker in northern California, which struck a partnership in 1997 with Hewlett Packard.

"There are a lot of players in the marketplace. The size of the problem is huge. No one vendor can solve all the problems by itself," says Todd Goldman, marketing manager for the Hewlett Packard (HP) OpenView system, which is used to develop operations support systems. HP has also developed an operations support system for wireless carriers. The system costs $3 million to $5 million, including hardware. It's a fully developed OSS that can be installed off the shelf, eliminating the months of work it takes to develop an OSS from scratch.

Carriers that don't want to bother creating their own OSS have an increasing number of options. Lucent Technologies, for example, launched an operations center in Denver that manages networks for local, long-distance and wireless companies. The center monitors its clients' networks and deploys new calling features. It's equipped to identify and repair problems on the network. Its first clients included ICG Communications and WinStar, the fixed-wireless carrier.

Managing Customer Relationships

Billing as marketing

MCI shook up the long-distance industry in 1991 with a new calling plan called Friends and Family. People who enrolled in the program received discounts on calls to a select circle of ten people. The program was a hit, elevating the image of a company known primarily as a cut-rate marketer. The sudden popularity of the program was a blow to

AT&T, which hadn't faced such a fierce fight in more than 100 years.

Friends and Family was targeted toward a market identified through careful analysis of long-distance calling patterns. It was executed with a sophisticated billing system that was able to separate routine traffic on the network from calls that belonged to a Friends and Family calling circle. It wasn't easy to duplicate.

It took AT&T nine months to craft the Call America plan and an additional six months to revamp its billing system for the new program. "By the time Call America came out, MCI had won valuable points in the market," says Jack Boyle, CEO of billing specialist Saville Systems. "Call America came out more than a year later, and the reason is that the information systems AT&T had weren't competitive with MCI."

It's a classic example of how billings plays a strategic role in telecommunications. "Billing used to be like a back-office application, and now it's become a strategic weapon to these telephone companies," Boyle says.

Billing systems are increasingly important. Telecommunications companies are evolving into carriers that offer four, five, or six services instead of just one. They are under pressure to design new services and rush them to market at warp speed—sometimes in a single day. They must develop strong customer relationships that will withstand powerful counteroffers from the competition. It all depends on a first-rate billing system.

Carriers expend an enormous amount of money and energy acquiring their customers, and they can't afford to let a competitor steal them. To recoup their investment and ultimately expand their business over a period of years, they need to keep their customers. That's why they are venturing into new markets. Customers are less likely to defect when they depend on a carrier for an elaborate combination of services. AT&T found that the retention rate among long-distance customers rose 20 percent when it sold them a Universal credit card, and that it rose 34 percent when it sold them wireless service. It expects retention rates to rise even higher when it adds a third, fourth, or fifth service to these "bundles."

Cross-discounting is another important marketing tool. A carrier will offer a discount on long-distance service to a subscriber who spends a certain amount of money on wireless service. Neither technique is possible without an open, flexible billing system that lends itself to quick implementation of new services. Competitors gain much by getting a new service or feature to market first because they can charge a premium price until the rest of the pack catches up.

Some companies take billing so seriously that they build their own billing system from scratch.

"All of this is tied to the billing system; it is the heart of the business," says Rick Davis, operations director at Network Long Distance in Newport News, Virginia. "You have to be able to bill your customers consistently and right every single billing cycle."

Network Long Distance has grown, through marketing and acquisitions, into a company with annual revenues of about $120 million. Davis started with Eastern Telecom, which was acquired by Network Long Distance in 1997. Eastern started out as a pay-phone company in 1989 and built a new billing system when it expanded into long-distance service. "We converted our existing billing system for pay phones into a long-distance configuration. We worked on it for six months," Davis adds.

Gene Chase was a computer programmer and consultant before he started Pantel, a small long-distance carrier. He helped another carrier automate a long-distance service, and that inspired him to launch his own network. Needless to say, Pantel runs its own billing system. "There's no way I could deal with an outside billing service. It's a core function, and we must maintain control of it," he says.

Those who lack the expertise to construct a billing system from scratch can hire a company to build one for them.

Saville has developed a convergent billing system, one that integrates numerous services onto a single bill and connects to the other computer systems that run a network. It serves middle- and larger-tier companies. Smaller carriers without the technical expertise to build their own system can farm out their billing to a service bureau, eliminating the need to construct a system at all. An outside company will handle the job for about $2 a bill, although bigger carriers that generate lots of volume can often negotiate a better price.

Small local phone companies typically spend 1 to 2 percent of their revenue on billing, says Scott Grill, of National Independent Billing. His 33-year-old company in Mankato, Minnesota got its start developing bills for small independent phone companies in northern Midwestern states such as Iowa, Wisconsin, and Minnesota. At one time that region had 300 small independent phone companies that weren't affiliated with the Bell System. The company began developing bills for the long-distance industry in the 1980s, following the breakup of AT&T. Now it handles bills for local phone ventures such as MCI Metro. But the basic function is the same. First, it retrieves the calling records from a telephone switch. That's often done by computer, although messengers are still used to fetch data from older switches. When the information is in hand, the billing company applies the phone company's basic rates to each customer's calls. Then it applies any existing discounts and taxes, and arrives at the customer's new balance.

For a long time, long-distance resellers chose from two kinds of bills: independent bills and bills that were combined with a customer's local phone bill. That difference is narrowing. Companies like National Independent Billing can now calculate an invoice and send the information along to another company, which will combine it with a local phone bill.

"It's the only ongoing communication between you and your customer," Grill says. "It has to be appealing. It has to be informative. It has to include the kind of information that will help your customers manage their communications." The bill creates a great opportunity for a company to distinguish itself. Working Assets, an affinity marketing company that targets politically active people on the left, includes the names of customers' local elected officials on its bills. An imaginative billing system can launch an entire business. Equitrac has a special billing system designed for law firms. Many carriers use billing systems to develop other types of niches. For example, a big corporate client that has offices in New York and Miami might want a special low rate for calls between those cities.

Many customers want to know detailed information on their calling habits: the number of calls, the average duration, the longest duration, the most frequently called numbers, the times of day when they place the most calls. And that information can be useful to the telecommunications company as well, because it contains extremely valuable demographic information. A good billing company can help a carrier figure out how many customers are buying a particular service, such as voice-mail. A special bill can be developed, targeting customers who don't already have a particular service.

Data warehousing

Offerings from communications companies are beginning to sound similar. Big and small companies alike are talking about offering bundles of four or five services that are marketed, operated, and billed as a group. This might still be a rather striking strategy—after all, few companies have fully implemented it. As 1997 drew to a close, few U.S. consumers could get local, long-distance, and wireless, let alone Internet access and television, on a single bill. That sort of one-stop shopping will probably be a routine matter in a few years, though. Carriers will have to try harder. The once-unassailable influence of established brands over the market is beginning to crumble, and competition has barely started, says analyst Bryan Van Dussen of The Yankee Group.

"To differentiate oneself, that proposition will have to increasingly reflect the key customers they are trying to attract," Van Dussen says. "It will have to speak to the needs and wants of the customer. The latest buzz words in the marketing departments of telecommunications companies are 'mass customization' and 'market of one,' which refers to designing services for individual customers."

Few organizations are up to the task, Van Dussen says. It will take a lot of work to even move in that direction. "To do that, you have to know your customers: how they behave, how they operate, how they eat, and how they sleep," he says. *Data warehousing* is one way to develop that knowledge. The data warehouse is a "central repository" of information that has been stripped from operating procedures, such as billing, and codified so it can be analyzed or accessed quickly from a desktop computer, Price Waterhouse says.

The creation of a data warehouse is a complex process that begins with extracting raw data from marketing, financial, and billings systems. It undergoes a process of filtering, cleaning, and summarizing, Price Waterhouse says. MCI's Friends and Family program is one example of a service created by analyzing this sort of customer data.

"MCI discovered a calling pattern between friends and families, and I don't have to take it much further than that," Van Dussen says. "Once they discovered it, they developed a product." MCI rolled out another example of a data warehouse-driven service in 1997. It documented that people like to spend Sunday on the phone, re-establishing ties with friends and family. So it created a feature that allows them to make long-distance calls on Sunday for 5 cents a minute. It's obvious that people like to call relatives on Sunday. You don't need a computer to tell you that. But you do need a computer to figure out exactly how big the market is and whether a 5-cent-a-minute rate is economically viable.

Communications products have traditionally been designed around technological platforms. Data warehousing allows companies to design new products and services around customers, and to create things that benefit the customer as well as the company.

"There is a tendency to see value creation as a supplier-centric thing," Van Dussen says. A company invests in an idea and seeks to profit from the sale of the resulting product. The new generation of products and services designed around customers allows them to derive value as well. AT&T refers to it as propelling the customers' business.

"The 800 market is an interesting example of one of the first attempts to diversify in the telecommunications business," Van Dussen says. "The customer buys it and then turns around and uses it to his own advantage." The toll-free phone number has become a fixture of business since AT&T created it 30 years ago. Now it's spreading into the residential market as well. For example, companies market 800 and 888 numbers as safety services to help kids stay in touch with their parents.

A new generation of services such as paging and short messaging creates more opportunities for companies to create services that their customers can capitalize upon. Just as companies used toll-free numbers to create 800-Flowers and other services, they can use digital technology to transmit news, stock prices, sports scores, and other customized information. The technology already exists. The key is developing applications that people actually want, and data warehousing is an important part of that project.

Call-centers

Ever receive a dinnertime call from a telemarketer? Then you know what a call-center is. It's a group of phone lines that link a company's employees to its customers. Call-centers grew out of the telephone customer service lines that airlines pioneered in the 1960s and 1970s, and now encompass a $500 billion economic sector, Price Waterhouse says. They have grown from a customer service medium to a crucial component of marketing, sales, public opinion surveys, and even political campaigns. Telecommunications companies use them to make unsolicited sales calls to millions of homes a year. Phone companies also set up call-centers for their clients. For example, a phone company can create a toll-free number for a catalog company, attend the lines 24 hours a day, process orders from customers, and prepare bills. Call-centers have been an entrepreneurial frontier for many big carriers that need to diversify beyond the sale of plain old telephone service.

Some companies have the resources to design and build their own call-center from scratch, but more and more carriers are buying prepacked hardware and software, says Tom Gormley, an analyst at Forrester Research. He says the bigger vendors include Vendros, Vantive, and Scopus. They target bigger carriers, but another group of companies is paying increasing attention to smaller carriers, making it possible for them to market in the manner of AT&T, MCI, and Sprint.

Remedy, Software Artistry, and Magic Solutions are some of the companies that have products for smaller players, according to Gormley. He says some entry-level systems are available for about $200,000. The larger systems—which must function across international boundaries and respond to more than one spoken language—cost millions.

There are two kinds of call-centers—inbound and outbound. Outbound call-centers are used for telemarketing. Inbound call-centers receive calls from customers, making them ideal for customer service lines and information lines.

A customer call to a phone company's center is typically intercepted by a device that answers the call, greets the customer, and gathers some basic information. A caller will be greeted with a voice-mail recording. Then, an integrated voice response system will ask a series of questions that the caller can answer by pressing buttons on his or her keypad. For example: *Press one to place an order; press two to talk to someone about your bill, press three for maintenance and repair.* This information is gathered by an automatic call distributor, which can tap a computer for additional information, such as the caller's address, repair history, and the special calling features he or she has ordered. More modern devices will replace the keypad response with voice recognition software that allows the caller to speak to the system. The automatic call-router assesses the data and sends the call to the next available agent or, better yet, to a specialist.

A message will appear on the agent's computer screen telling him or her to pick up the phone. The automatic call-router will send all the information it has gathered about the caller to the agent's computer screen. The sudden appearance of the data is known as a *screen pop.*

Sophisticated call-centers lend themselves to entrepreneurial organizations. Every time a customer calls, a company with good technology can assess what services that person has, and an enterprising employee can sell them more. "There is a cross-selling and up-selling opportunity that most call-centers don't take advantage of," Gormley says. This requires top technology and top employees who are cross-trained as customer service representatives and sales agents. It's a perfect example of why companies must break down rigid bureaucracies and job descriptions to succeed in a competitive telecommunications market.

"Call-centers have historically been a substantial, albeit necessary cost," says Gary Hickof, global marketing vice president for AT&T Networked Commerce Services. "We are leading customers to think of call-centers as profit centers. Customer care and telemarketing are not mutually exclusive."

Moving to the Web

Forrester Research says call-centers can increase their efficiency and expand their channels of influence by expanding from the telephone to the Web, where they have been slow to build a presence. A "rising tide of e-mails is headed toward the call-center, but it will take two years for the tools needed to manage them to catch up," Forrester Research said in its February 1997 edition of *Telecom Strategies*. "The Web will come to life as call-center agents gain the flexibility to share screens with customers and talk to them at the same time." AT&T WorldNet customers already have the ability to push a button on the service's Web site to request a phone call from a customer service agent.

Call-centers will evolve into customer-interaction centers that include the Internet and e-mail, Forrester Research says. Companies such as Webline are already pushing the industry in that direction. Webline allows a customer service agent to take control of a customer's computer screen, pushing product information, reviews, or pictures onto the customer's Web browser.

"We have added a visual component to telemarketing. I can actually take control of your browser and add anything I want to the screen, record whatever is going on, and complete a sale," Webline president Pasha Roberts says. "We're using phones and the Internet together." The system, based on Java technology, can be applied to sales, customer service, or teleconferencing. Target markets: financial companies and possibly travel companies.

Call-centers can start moving to the Web by taking these steps, Forrester Research says:

[*] Shift to e-mail and World Wide Web communications when appropriate. Use e-mail for non-urgent communications. E-mail requests for certain types of standard information, such as a list of rates or services, can be answered automatically if the requests are standardized with the use of e-mail forms. That will cut labor costs and allow employees to focus on more complex problems.

[*] Develop multimedia e-mail marketing campaigns as an alternative to printed catalogs.

- Target big spenders with "teleweb" capabilities.

- Cut costs by using cheap network computers instead of PCs.

- Staff your call-center with college educated people with good writing and Internet skills.

Customer Relationship Marketing

Telephone companies didn't even have marketing depart-ments in the 1960s. They had something known as "de-partments of revenue requirements," says Bob Atkins, a vice president at Mercer Management Consulting. The world has changed so much that few people today could even be-gin to imagine what a department of revenue requirements might do. Then again, there probably weren't any telephone executives 30 years ago who could have imagined how their jobs would change.

The conception of the customer has changed radically during the last three decades, Atkins says. The protected phone monopolies of the 1960s didn't have to worry about competition. Everyone needed a phone, and they didn't have a choice in where to obtain it. The company figured out its costs, added a return on its investment, and developed prices that would meet those needs. Then it told the public what it needed to do to obtain phone service. Advertising and public relations functions were there to explain the process to the public, present a positive face, and sway the regulators and lawmakers, who really controlled the company's destiny.

It wasn't that the companies didn't care about their customers. To the contrary, the phone companies provided nearly flawless service to the great majority of the public at a relatively affordable rate. The company also responded quickly when disaster struck and service was disrupted. Despite this strong "ethic of service," the company still thought of its customers as "a vehicle for utilizing the products and services the phone companies wanted to sell," Atkins says.

The company was organized in a rigid hierarchical fashion to deliver a few products to the mass market. It probably had more in common with the Army Corps of Engineers than it did with today's looser business structures. The competitive market requires an entirely different business model. For one thing, it's organized around the customer, not the product. This change is part of a broad trend that has rippled through the economy from one industry to another, Mercer says.

From automobiles to financial services to telecom, the old measures of success are being replaced, Mercer says. Efficiency, productivity, and lowest-cost production don't guarantee success. Companies are now rising and falling with the quality of their "customer relationship marketing," the management of the customer's experience before the sale, during the sale, and after the sale.

"There isn't anyone in telecommunications who isn't working on this right now, figuring out how to cement these relationships and who to cement them with," Atkins says. "It's very much the game now."

It's a high-stakes game, too. Mercer says a major shareholder-value migration is underway in telecommunications. It's "stable to growing" among the local exchange carriers. It's declining among long-distance carriers, and growing rapidly among nontraditional players such as competitive local exchange carriers, satellite carriers, microwave carriers, data companies, and cable TV companies. Companies must work harder to keep their customers at a volatile time. The competition is out there.

Mercer says the benchmark for profitable growth through customer relationships has been set outside of telecommunications. For a good example in a related field, though, he cites Dell Computer. Mercer says Dell had two fundamental insights in the 1980s: (1) It realized many customers weren't first-time buyers, and (2) it decided that many of these customers knew more about computers than did the sales forces in many retail outlets.

Dell concluded that a good percentage of the market was ready to buy directly from the manufacturer. It build a mail-order business that turned the manufacturing and sales process upside down. Instead of building a computer, shipping it to a reseller, and waiting for a sale, Dell enticed customers to place an order directly. Then it built the machine to order and shipped it to the customer. The company built customer profiles that shaped its product development and its identification in the market.

The catalog industry has also learned to segment its market. Companies that distributed a single catalog ten years ago now distribute a dozen different catalogs to carefully targeted groups of customers. "It's not rocket science, but it's way more sophisticated than the telecom players (are used to)," says Mercer vice president Bob Fox. "They want to get there, but it's difficult. It's going to become more important as these (telecommunications) companies think about offering multiple services, because the mixture of these services varies more with each individual customer."

Atkins and Fox suggest a few steps that telecom companies can take:

Look beyond the obvious for new markets: Telecom companies typically pursue high-volume customers—those who spend lots of money. These segments of the market are increasingly competitive. The margins have been bid out of them in many cases. It often makes more sense to pursue groups of customers that don't appear quite as desirable, and then figure out a way to build a profitable relationship. Many smaller telecom carriers are offering prepaid local, long-distance, and wireless services to customers who have poor credit, or no credit, and don't qualify for regular service. Credit risk is eliminated because these customers pay for their service in advance. These services often command a premium price. Dial-around services target an obscure market, too. These companies allow people to dial a code and bypass their regular long-distance carrier for a particular call.

Dial-around companies don't bill their customers directly, avoiding a major fixed cost of doing business. They also avoid paying access charges. "You might not be a high-volume user, but the dial-around companies can still make money on you," Atkins says. An added benefit: The customer's regular carrier has no idea that the customer is using another carrier, so it can't launch a counter-marketing strategy.

Stay on the cutting edge of technology: High speed services such as cable modems and digital subscriber lines satisfy a growing customer demand. "Be at the cutting edge in terms of high speed and low cost. There will always be an appetite for the lowest-cost bit in high volumes," Atkins says. Customers are also looking for ways to combine their rapidly growing arsenals of wireless phones, pagers, fax machines, computers, and voice mail boxes. "None of these companies have quite figured out how to combine them," Fox says.

Create tiers: Separate customers into tiers, as credit-card companies do. Identify "platinum" or "gold" customers and give them special treatment.

Understand how much a given customer is likely to spend in the future: One of the newest ideas in relationship marketing is *net present value*. Companies are figuring out how much a particular customer is likely to spend in the future, adjusting the amount for variables such as inflation, and then calculating how much that customer is worth in *present dollars*. Then the company figures out how much it is willing to spend on that customer. The information is stored in a data warehouse available to customer service representatives. When that customer calls and asks for a discount—such as a lower long-distance rate or a free wireless phone—the company can make an informed decision about what it should invest in the relationship.

"Net present value is at a medium state of development in telecommunications," Fox says. "Three years ago, it was not out there."

There are limits to the value of these calculations, though. It's difficult to predict just how much money a customer will spend in an emerging market or medium like the Internet.

Marketing in the Age of the Internet

Telecommunications companies share a new burden with the rest of the world: learning to communicate in the age of the Internet. Business-to-business sales on the Internet will undergo explosive growth during the next few years. These sales accounted for $8 billion worth of goods and services in 1997, and their value will hit $327 billion in 2002, Calico Technology says, citing a report by Forrester Research.

Backed by venture-capital powerhouse Kleiner Perkins Caufield & Byers, Calico is a three-year-old software company in San Jose, California, that creates shopping systems for the Web. Companies such as Dell Computer and Cisco Systems have used Calico software to create Web pages that allow their customers to configure, quote, and order complex products. Dell's Web site, for example, allows computer customers to figure out what options they want, add up the price of the components, and order a complete system.

Calico CEO Alan Naumann says business's *real* Year-2000 problem is a marketing problem, not a computer-calendar problem. Technology allows suppliers to create a vast number of carefully targeted products. And that's confusing the customer. Calico's products are designed to help customers choose and buy products, to help them shop in a complicated Web environment. Even the once-simple task of ordering a cup of coffee has become a complex task in a world of Starbucks coffee bars: *Americano? Will that be the house blend or a coffee of the day? Short, tall, or grande? Latte or cappuccino? Skim milk or whole milk? Sugar?* Telecom companies are learning to segment their market just the way Starbucks has done so profitably. But that segmentation creates new challenges.

"Customer confusion delays their product decisions," says Naumann, 37, a veteran of Hewlett Packard and Cadence software. "Traditional sales and marketing approaches become ineffectual. How do you maintain intimacy in the face of exploding complexity?"

Intimacy in a coffee bar isn't so hard to imagine. But how do you create intimacy between an anonymous buyer and seller on the Web? He has several suggestions for telecom companies:

- Allow customers to download samples of the products and services, such as voice-mail or the latest digital wireless technology. Let them hear the new service, or view the latest video-conferencing technique.

- Let them calculate a sample bill that demonstrates how much money they would have saved using the latest price plan.

- Create a *chat room* where customers can discuss a company's products and services. The company will gain valuable insights into customer attitudes. And customers will appreciate independent opinions about the product.

⊡ Offer a higher level of service. For example, a utility
company might warn customers in California that El
Niño is coming and offer to trim tree branches that are
brushing against utility lines.

And remember to smile and say *thank-you!*

There is no substitute for the fundamentals of service,
for sheer effort on behalf of the customer. "We called it
customer service fanaticism," former MFS president Royce
Holland recalls. MFS had technicians on call 24-hours a
day. Customers could summon help whenever they needed
it; MFS people thought nothing of getting out of bed at 2
a.m. to answer a call, says Holland, now chairman and CEO
of Allegiance Telecom in Dallas. Nothing beats this story,
though:

MFS was constructing the network in Baltimore in 1990.
The cable splicing wasn't moving along quickly enough for
a manager, who was watching the construction crews do
their job. The man jumped into a manhole full of water,
business suit and all, to help the workers meet their deadline.

Case Studies

Case Studies

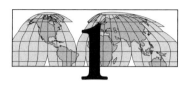

David McCourt and RCN
*Laying local fiber
in the residential market*

As entrepreneurs across the country race to construct local phone networks for businesses, David McCourt is betting $7 billion that the biggest opportunity lies with consumers.

The very notion of building a new local network to compete with the regional Bells has been synonymous with the business market from the beginning ten years ago. McCourt himself pioneered local competition in the 1980s by constructing local networks for businesses in Boston, where he teamed up with MFS and Peter Kiewit & Sons. Other companies, such as Teleport Communications and Brooks Fiber, built local networks in the medium to large business markets around the country.

McCourt's new venture, Residential Communications Network (RCN), is the only competitive local exchange carrier in the country to target consumers. His fiber-optic local loops are designed to carry local and long-distance

David McCourt

voice service, high-speed Internet access, and cable television programming.

"The growth is on the residential side and all around the Internet," says the 40-year-old entrepreneur, who spun RCN off of C-TEC Corp. in September 1997. "Today, we think of voice, video, and data as separate services. Ten years from now, it will all be data, even though it might appear on your screen as video. It will all be transported through packet routing."

Taking advantage of the convergence created by data, McCourt is pursuing big opportunities selling a combination of services to consumers connected to his fiber-optic networks. The business market has been attractive because it allows carriers to concentrate great numbers of high-spending customers in a small geographic area. That allows them to squeeze lots of revenue out of their networks, which have a one-time fixed construction cost. Residential customers are generally dispersed over a wider area, and they don't spend as much money as businesses do. But McCourt studied the residential market in the Northeast and saw some similarities to the business market. The Northeast corridor between Boston and Washington concentrates 28 percent of the U.S. population in just 4 percent of the country's geographic area. The average household income is 16 percent higher than the nationwide average, too.

McCourt narrowed his focus even further—to the Northeast's 24 markets, all of which have at least 300,000 people. Estimated revenue in the region is $10 billion a year. RCN began constructing the sort of fiber-optic local networks that businesses have been enjoying for the last decade. Phone companies traditionally use two-way copper wires that carry 64,000 kilobits a second of information. Cable companies traditionally use a combination of coaxial cable and fiber-optic cable that carries millions of bits a second. But it's designed as a one-way system that carries information to the customer, not the other way. Cable companies are designing their networks for high-speed Internet access, but only a limited number of customers can obtain the highest speeds at once, because they share the transmission lines. McCourt is building networks that use a higher proportion of fiber. That allows customers to download files from the Internet at 10 megabits a second, regardless of how many other people in the neighborhood are using the system at the same time. "RCN's network… has enormous capacity, not unlike the fiber networks of the

long-distance carriers," analyst Bruce Roberts, of SBC
Warburg Dillon Read, said in a September 1997 report.

McCourt cut his construction costs by forming a joint
venture with Boston Edison Co. in Boston, which operates
a 200-mile fiber-optic network that runs by the homes of
1.6 million people. He struck a similar agreement with the
Potomac Electric Power Co., which operates a 350-mile
fiber network in greater Washington. "By 2007, we expect
RCN to have 2.4 million cable TV subscribers, 2.6 million
local telephone customers, and 400,000 local business telephone customers," Roberts says.

As 1997 ended, RCN was offering cable and phone service to nearly 100,000 customers in New York, Washington, and Boston. Using a combination of his fiber-optic
networks, traditional cable systems, and local phone resale,
McCourt was taking on Bell Atlantic, Time-Warner, and
CableVision Systems with a $10 million advertising cam-
paign that portrayed the competition as Soviet-style em-
pires. It had access agreements with more than 400 affluent
residential buildings that received service over its fiber-optic cables. McCourt plans to roll out one new market every
three months for the next two years.

He will face plenty of competition, though. Cablevision,
which has 3.2 million cable TV customers in Boston, New
York, and Cleveland, is preparing to carry phone service
and high speed Internet access. It's already offering advanced
services on Long Island, New York. Bell Atlantic, which
plans to offer high-speed digital modems throughout its territory, says it will build a series of fiber-optic networks, too,
beginning with Philadelphia in 1998.

In the meantime, RCN also operates a competitive cable
TV system in Pennsylvania's Lehigh Valley, one of the few
cable companies in the country to face competition from
another carrier. Cash flow has increased to $1.2 million a
month from $300,000 a month since RCN bought it. RCN
also operates an international division that owns 40 percent
of Mexico's second largest cable TV company.

An Accidental Strategy

McCourt's strategy of building his own local networks evolved by accident. He originally planned to lease capacity on the networks of MFS, his former partner. The idea was that RCN would add traffic to the networks during the evening, supplementing the heavy daytime traffic of the businesses on MFS's network. The deal would have cut RCN's capital requirements in half. But something went wrong: MFS was using twice as much fiber capacity as it expected, and it couldn't spare enough to meet RCN's needs. It was 1995 and the Internet was just beginning to surge in popularity among consumers and businesses.

McCourt panicked at first. But then he began to reconsider the idea that he couldn't afford to build his own networks. If demand for MFS's network was so strong, then it should support a new network, too. He's happy now that the MFS deal didn't work out.

McCourt is a builder by nature. It's in his blood. He grew up in an Irish family with seven children in Watertown, Massachusetts, the son and grandson of major contractors. McCourt originally wanted to be a policeman. He studied sociology at Georgetown University, and entertained thoughts of becoming a social worker, working as a parole officer's assistant in Washington. His life changed one summer after college. McCourt was doing construction work for his father and noticed a news story that derided Cablevision's plan to build one of the first urban cable TV systems in Boston. Conventional wisdom at the time dictated that cable couldn't be done in the city. McCourt called on Cablevision CEO Chuck Dolan and promised to build the system by a certain date. He got the job.

A dispute arose between Cablevision and McCourt. McCourt says the episode changed the direction of his life. The young entrepreneur was forced to cut his expenses while he waited to get paid. One night, McCourt was at the Sevens, a pub on Beacon Hill in Boston. He was the youngest member of a regular group that included developer Donald

Chiofaro, who built International Place, the tallest building in the city. Tom O'Neill, son of House Speaker Tip O'Neill, was there, too.

The O'Neill and McCourt families had known each other for years. David McCourt had even spent a summer working for Tip O'Neill. When McCourt needed advice on how to convince Boston officials to approve his contract with Cablevision, he turned to Tip's son, Tom O'Neill, for political counsel. Much of that help was received during regular meetings at the Sevens.

McCourt says he received a valuable lesson from Chiofaro there, too.

McCourt was complaining to the group about his dispute with Cablevision one night, and Chiofaro grew tired of the younger developer's whining. So Chiofaro, a former Harvard football player, leaned across the table, grabbed McCourt by the necktie, and bit him on the nose, McCourt relates.

"Chiofaro must have had enough," says O'Neill, now a partner with public relations firm McDermott/O'Neill. "He said, 'if somebody bothers you, David, this is what you do.'"

Chiofaro denies the incident occured, but McCourt swears it's true.

Showdown with Cablevision

McCourt swears the story is true, and that he has never been able to tolerate whining since then.

Soon after the incident, McCourt forced a showdown with Cablevision by digging up a section of its TV cable. When the problem was finally resolved, McCourt found himself with a lean, debt-free business and a lot of cash. He used the money to launch Corporate Communications Network, bypassing Nynex's local phone network by providing businesses a direct discount link to their long-distance carrier.

MFS was offering a similar service in Chicago and the two companies merged operations into MFS/McCourt in

1988. McCourt ran the Boston operation for several years along with a television station in Grenada. He went to Grenada to build an airfield runway shortly after the U.S. invasion, and he decided to stay a few years and help restore television service to the country. McCourt brought college students in from the United States to run the station in return for course credit, and he housed them in the former Cuban embassy. He also sent students from Grenada to the United States, training them to eventually run the station.

McCourt went to England next, where he operated cable television and local phone networks with Peter Kiewit & Sons, the Omaha-based construction company that had funded MFS. McCourt returned to the United States in the early 1990s and set his sights on the local market. He bought C-Tec, a local phone and cable company based in Princeton, New Jersey.

C-Tec included Commonwealth Telephone, an independent phone company with 240,000 lines, and Michigan Cable, with 200,000 customers. He established a new C-Tec division to compete with other local phone companies in the U.S. markets, which appeared to be on the verge of dismantling old residential monopolies. And that was the beginning of Residential Communications Network.

Christopher Hartnett and USA Global Link

International Internet telephony

Christopher Hartnett was in a hotel room in the little town of Heinsburg, in Holland, near the German border. It was September 10, 1997, and he had been on the road almost continuously for nearly a year. He was traveling around the world recruiting sales representatives and partners for his company, USA Global Link. The venture was conceived just four years before amid the cornfields of Fairfield, Iowa.

The idea was simple: provide an alternative to the ridiculously high prices that many of the world's phone monopolies charged for international service. Callers in Singapore or Indonesia, for example, dialed a toll-free number that connected them to USA Global Link. They hung up after the first ring, which gave the company enough time to identify the number of the incoming call. The company's

Christopher Hartnett

switch placed an automated call to the person overseas, who heard a cheaper U.S. dial tone when he or she picked up the phone. That allowed the person to place an international call at the cheaper U.S. rate.

This clever game was fabulously lucrative for USA Global Link and other "call-back" companies. USA Global Link was generating at least $500 million a year in revenue as Hartnett spoke from Holland. It's a game of arbitrage, meaning that it exploits the fact that one product or service can command different prices in different markets. Like all arbitrages, this one contained the seeds of its own destruction, Hartnett said. International carriers were lowering their prices in response to the competition. That decline in price accelerated in 1997 when 70 countries around the world signed a treaty promising to open their phone markets to competition.

Hartnett never viewed USA Global Link as a call-back company, though. He saw it as a discount phone company. As the call-back market passed its peak, Hartnett was piecing together a new and potentially more powerful strategy based on the Internet. His latest vision is to construct a $500 million Internet-based global communications network that will carry voice, data, and electronic commerce.

Harnett was working furiously to get the new global business off the ground, meeting with Internet service providers around the world. He had been to Switzerland, France, Germany, the Netherlands, England, Belgium, Singapore, Taiwan, Korea, and Hong Kong during the previous two months. He had been home just three days during the previous December and six days during January. His wife and three daughters were traveling with him now, and Harnett said that the youngest, age four, could sing "Happy Birthday" in seven languages.

Hartnett says customers won't need computers to use the new Internet-based service. They will dial a toll-free number that patches them into the company's network. It will travel over USA Global Link's own network of routers, so it won't have to compete with other traffic on the Internet. USA Global Link is building its own routers, and it will install its own fiber as well. The call will be handed off to a local phone company for completion.

The network will carry voice and data services and more than 20 other services, from fax on demand to banking and commodity trading. Hartnett plans to construct USA Global

Link office buildings around the world, where customers can do business.

Hartnett still owns 34 percent of the company. PT Indosat owns 20 percent, and a group of private investors in Chicago own the rest. But the company plans a high-yield debt offering and a stock offering. Hartnett said he was working with four investment banks—Merrill Lynch, Morgan Stanley, Goldman Sachs, and CS First Boston.

"Our five-year projections show us at $25 billion (in revenue)," he says. "We got out in the world and we realized... we could quickly become a multi-multi-billion dollar company. The barriers to competition were not all that great, and if one had a global focus, one could make a lot of money."

Singapore Jail Threat

One big risk is that the global governments, protective of the cash-rich phone businesses, will try to crush Internet telephony just as they tried to crush international call-back. Hartnett says a Singapore Telephone executive once threatened to jail him. The executive invited him to Singapore in 1994 to discuss a possible business arrangement, Hartnett says. He recalled sitting down at a big boardroom table as the executive told him that he had stolen $300 million from Singapore.

"He told me he could have me put in jail in 15 minutes," Hartnett recalled. "He told me I had cost his country $300 million, that he had to lower rates three times in 1994 to compete with USA Global Link. I told him we had saved his people $300 million." The executive informed Hartnett that he was lucky he wasn't in Indonesia, unaware that Indosat would soon invest in Hartnett's company. Singapore Telephone did not respond to requests for interviews for this book.

Several countries have already cracked down on Internet phone service, but Hartnett says the company's geographic diversity will help protect it. It plans to operate in 120 countries.

Hartnett grew up in Chicago and New York, the son of builder Bill Hartnett, who constructed Lake Point Towers in Chicago and the U.N. Plaza in Manhattan. He worked as an international gem stone importer and as a trader at the Chicago Mercantile Exchange. He became fascinated with international call-back during a business trip to Southeast Asia, where he tried it himself. He raised $7.5 million from private investors to get a call-back business of his own off the ground. It began operations in October 1992. It had revenue of $241 million in 1996, and it was pushing $500 million in 1997. Hartnett says the run rate at the end of 1997—the amount of annual revenue the company would generate if it kept that pace for an entire year—was close to $1 billion.

Hartnett says he works 16 to 22 hours a day. He offsets the work with the "deep rest" that he achieves twice a day from the practice of transcendental meditation (TM). He became a meditator during his college years at Loyola Marymount University in Los Angeles. He transferred during his senior year to Maharishi University in Santa Barbara—the very same day that the school bought Parsons College in Fairfield. He spent an additional four years attending courses in Iowa, earning an undergraduate degree in business. He also holds a doctorate in business management from Maharishi University.

Hartnett seems slightly annoyed with questions about his meditation. He would rather talk business. "It's not a religion. It's not a cult," he sighs. "I think it makes (me) more coherent and rested. That's all TM does."

Not quite satisfied that the subject has been settled, he offers one more point. "People get all bent out of shape about the TM, but no one is walking around (the offices) in robes. Let it be known that we are into making money, into making a lot of it."

Joe Nacchio and Qwest

Building the new long-distance network

Qwest announced in August 1997 that it was realigning its budding nationwide long-distance network around the Internet and Silicon Valley. One week later, the young company's stock had added $1 billion in market value.

Qwest's strategy is designed to take advantage of two of the most important forces in today's telecommunications market:

1. Its $2.4 billion plan to build 17,000 miles of high capacity fiber across the United States and Mexico reflects a shortage on existing networks. "We view Qwest as simply the right asset at the right time in the telecom industry, given the exploding demand for bandwidth and the ever-increasing strains on capacity," Salomon Smith Barney wrote in a September 1997 report. The investment bank noted that capacity utilization in the long-distance industry hit 80 to 85 percent in 1997, up from

Joe Nacchio

just over 30 percent in 1989. The solution: build more fiber networks.

2. Qwest's decision to equip those cables with Internet routers as well as traditional voice switches shows how telecommunications is redefining itself around data. Data traffic is growing 20 times faster than voice, and the average Internet message takes up to 4,000 times as much bandwidth as the average voice call, Salomon says.

"Ultimately, voice becomes an application on this network where everything is encoded digits and it's all packet-routed," Qwest CEO Joe Nacchio says. The Brooklyn-born executive left AT&T in late 1996 after 26 years. His last position was executive vice president for the company's consumer and small business division. Nacchio was a marketing specialist at AT&T, but his obsession at Qwest appears to be technology. The early traffic on Qwest's network is half data, half voice, although Nacchio expects data to comprise 90 percent of the traffic before too long. He also expects most of that data to be managed with Internet routers, instead of other systems. "We are going to push our product development along the lines of (the) Internet… because that is where we think the future's going."

The company was launched by Philip Anschutz, a Denver-based billionaire who made his fortune in railroads. Anschutz owned Southern Pacific Railroad and a subsidiary, Southern Pacific Construction, which built structures for tenants who wanted to run businesses along the railroad lines. Anschutz figured he could construct businesses for himself just as easily, and that decision gave rise to Qwest. He has sold Southern Pacific to Union Pacific, but Qwest's roots are clear. About 85 percent of the network's fiber-optic lines have been laid in railroad beds. The rest lie beneath public highways, such as the New York State Thruway.

Nacchio, who began his career as a lineman with New York Telephone, is still enthusiastic about the construction side of the business, which is reminiscent of the building of the railroads that literally paved the way for the communications network. Workers are stringing 48 cables across North America, passing 125 of its top markets. "We have 2,000 people on any given day building this network. Everywhere we go, we put conduits in the ground and a manhole every mile, and we put cable through it," Nacchio says. "As we speak, we have a crew in the Pacific Northwest building through mountains. We have a crew in the Southwest building between San Diego and Yuma, New Mexico."

The pace varies. Crews working in the Plains states can lay 250 miles of cable in a week. Workers blasting through mountains might advance 200 or 300 yards a day. They are scheduled to finish the job in mid-1999.

Nacchio says the network's advanced glass cable and data compression technology are key. Fiber-optic cables transmit information as flashes of light along a thin glass cable. The idea of using light to transmit information goes back to Alexander Graham Bell, who developed a prototype that ran on sunlight. The first generation of commercial long-distance fiber-optic networks appeared in the 1980s. The technology has advanced since then. Older cables carried flashes of light at a single wavelength, or color.

Qwest's cables have eight windows, or streams of light operating with different colors. Each color stream within the fiber carries about 10 gigabits of information. The division of the cable into multiple lanes is achieved by a compression technique known as *wavelength division multiplexing*. It's still evolving. The next generation of fiber will have 16 windows, each capable of carrying 40 gigabits of information a second. These lines command a high price in a world short of network capacity.

Twenty Times the 'Throughput'

"Long-haul fiber capacity is the tightest it's been in 20 years," Salomon Smith Barney says. Qwest's fiber can help meet that demand. It will have less than half the physical fiber of AT&T, which has a 41,000-mile network. Yet Qwest could theoretically have 20 times the "throughput," assuming that all of its network is put to use, Salomon says.

The second big technological issue is traffic control. That's traditionally been the job of the telephone switch, which directs a call from one phone to another and maintains a separate lane of traffic for each call. Newer forms of technology break the call into digitized bits of information, which travel in one big lane instead of separate lanes, or circuits. These "packets" are coded with their destination.

Computers known as routers read the codes and send the packets along their way. They don't always arrive at quite the same time, which explains why voice over the Internet often hasn't worked as well as voice over the telephone circuit.

The Internet is simply one standard, or protocol, of packet-data transmission. There are others, such as frame relay or Asynchronous Transfer Mode (ATM). Many people believed that frame relay or ATM would gain the upper hand, because they're supposedly higher quality systems. But the Internet protocol (IP) gained momentum on an almost daily basis during 1997. It's an open, publicly available standard used by 30 million people. The Internet, and its offspring the World Wide Web, have become a *de facto* standard for government, academic, and business communication around the world. The value of a network standard rises as more people adopt it.

Qwest's Network is loaded with Nortel voice switches and Cisco Internet routers. It will probably offer some frame relay and maybe some ATM service to serve its customers. But the big bet is on the Internet.

"We will push our product development along the lines of native IP routers," Nacchio says. He signed a product development agreement with Cisco in August 1997, and he's pushing the company to make routers that can process gigabits and even terabits of information in a single second.

Wall Street has thrown its money behind Qwest. "One week after Qwest said it was going to the IP protocol, its market value went up $1 billion," says Bob Atkins, a consultant at Mercer Management.

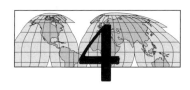

Alex Mandl and Teligent

A wireless connection to the office

The weeks after Alex Mandl's surprise departure from AT&T were filled with uncertainty for the high-profile executive. His decision to step down as president of the country's largest telecommunications company and join a start-up wireless venture caused enough of a buzz. But this was heightened even more by speculation over AT&T's fascinating internal politics. Mandl had no guarantee that he would ever succeed then-chairman and CEO Bob Allen. And then there was the issue of Mandl's pay. Associated Communications lured him with a $20 million signing bonus and the chance to make hundreds of millions more if he launched a successful initial public offering for his new employer. That's a lot of money, even considering the high pay that CEOs command these days.

The drama was also driven by Mandl's personality and reputation. He comes across as the epitome of the self-assured executive. The carefully tailored suits hang perfectly on his stocky frame. The Austrian-accented baritone voice exudes authority. The eyes, shrouded by heavy lids, lock on their subject with hardly a blink. There is a decisive air about him. This is the chief executive who doubled the revenues of shipper Sealand Services between 1988 to 1991. Mandl also led AT&T's $11.5 billion acquisition of McCaw Cellular Communications, the world's largest wireless phone company. It now appears that Mandl has a sense of humor, too. And he needed it to survive some of the bumps during the last year.

Yet even before the hype died down, Mandl found himself alone in a plain office in suburban Virginia. The business consisted of nothing but an idea, some radio licenses, and some money. It was up to him to bring the rest to life, and it wasn't about to fall into place in deference to his past. He had to put his cuff links on one at a time, so to speak. "I walked out of AT&T and I took a week or so off, and then got hold of Rajendra Singh, who owns Telcom Ventures," says Mandl, now 53. "I said, I need to borrow a little office for a few weeks. He gave me an office in his complex (in northern Virginia) and I sat down and said, 'What do I do next?'"

Associated, now known as Teligent, is controlled by Myles Berkman, the son of a greeting card magnate who had diversified into radio and cable television in the 1960s and 1970s. Singh, the head of Telcom Ventures and investor in LCC International, owned the rest. They wanted to provide businesses with high-speed voice, data, and video communications over two-way microwave radio systems. They planned to deploy non-mobile, or "fixed" wireless phones, that are tethered to a wall socket and connected to an antenna on the top of an office building's rooftop. The antenna transmits the signal to Teligent collection points, which send it along to its destination on voice or data networks around the world. Fixed wireless is new to the United States, but it's relatively common in other countries such as England. The entire system is designed to bypass the local phone networks of established players like the regional Bells and GTE. Mandl says they still control 98 percent of the local market.

As 1997 drew to a close, the organizational phase of Teligent was drawing to a close. Mandl had raised $100 million from Nippon Telegraph & Telephone, and he was preparing for an initial public offering. He was about to begin operations in the first of 74 markets. Mandl paused to reflect on some of the issues that he had confronted during the first 12 months: recruiting a team, sharpening the business plan, and working with the government to resolve competing claims for the radio spectrum that he planned to use. And he had to find a permanent office.

A Spectrum Dispute

The spectrum dispute was one of those unexpected crises that every entrepreneur should learn to expect. Mandl planned to use the 18 gigaherz frequency. Teledesic, the satellite venture backed by Bill Gates and Craig McCaw, said Teligent would interfere with its transmissions. The government had claims on the spectrum, too, so the FCC arranged a settlement. Teledesic stayed at the 18 gigaherz band and Teligent moved to 24 gigaherz, picking up a bigger piece of the airwaves in exchange for its trouble. BellSouth, Hughes Electronics, and other companies have complained about the FCC's decision to give Teligent more spectrum, but Mandl says the issue is essentially settled.

"We had this little debate with Teledesic early on. It was a bit of a distraction for a couple of months. The government wanted to get that resolved," Mandl says. "Frankly, our preference was to stay at eighteen. It probably cost us a couple months, but once we got through that we really started building the team."

Mandl was looking for a mix of smart people, but he focused on recruiting executives who had experience competing in the local phone market. "One of the things I learned at AT&T is that the long-distance business is very different from local service... The issues in the local market are very different," he says. The operating systems, regulations, and dealings with the dominant local phone companies are unique.

He met one of his key hires by accident. Mandl was on a commercial flight next to a passenger with a horrible cold. He asked the flight attendant if he could change seats, but the plane was full and Mandl was stuck. He settled back into his seat, only to be interrupted by his pager a moment later. "I'll be damned!" Mandl said as he read the message. "The guy leaned over and asked, 'What's that?'" Mandl told him that British Telecommunications had just announced plans to buy MCI.

He was sharing the row with Buddy Pickle, a senior marketing executive at local telephone upstart MFS Communications. Pickle, 40, had cut his teeth at AT&T in Atlanta, where he was known to fuel all-night work sessions by brewing double-strength coffee.

When Mandl met with a headhunter a few days later to review a list of people that might help them build the company, Pickle's name happened to be at the top. "I said I just met this man last week, and by the way, I'm sick as a dog," Mandl recalls. They met for dinner and Pickle signed on as president.

Mandl and Pickle hired a prominent group of people to help them run the company. They tapped MCI regulatory expert Larry Harris as senior vice president and general counsel. Keith Kaczmarek, head of engineering at Sprint's PCS PrimeCo venture, came aboard as senior vice president for engineering and operations. Richard Hanna, former CEO of MFS's small and medium-size business unit, Intelenet, was hired as senior vice president for marketing and sales. "In almost all cases, we were able to attract our first choice. I think that's because the opportunity we have is one people found fascinating," Mandl says. "And so, slowly but surely we built a team. In the end, you are only going to be as good as the team you pull together."

The next order of business was to refine Teligent's plan. The broad outlines of the business were clear, but many questions had to be settled: How would the company make the most of its opportunity? What vendors should it choose? What approach should it take to marketing and sales? Should it enter the wholesale or retail market or both? Exactly what sort of customer did the company want? "I happen to believe that the more focused you can be, the better chance you have to build a terrific business," Mandl says.

He believed he would have to choose between the wholesale and retail markets. It's difficult to function as a wholesale supplier when clients know you might be competing against them at the retail level. So Mandl focused the business on retail for a number of reasons.

- The economics are better. The local business market produces margins of 50 percent at the retail level.

- Wholesalers often rely on a few large clients, leaving them vulnerable if one defects to another supplier.

- Wholesalers face natural limits on the range of partnerships. It's difficult to strike an alliance with AT&T if you are already a major supplier to Sprint.

Smaller Businesses Targeted

Teligent targeted small and medium-size businesses. The Fortune 500, Mandl says, were already well-served with an array of services and competitive prices. "It's the next 5 million customers that tend to be under-served," he said. "That's where we see the much better opportunity."

Small and medium-size businesses account for about two-thirds of the $110 billion business market for local, long-distance, wireless, and data communications, Mandl says. Teligent says the market is growing quickly. Local and long-distance are about $45 billion each. Cellular accounts for $8 billion, and data accounts for $10 billion. Voice is growing 6 percent to 10 percent a year, cellular is growing

30 percent a year, and data is growing 25 percent to 30 percent.

Teligent faces competition from fixed wireless carriers such as WinStar and new companies that will buy licenses to operate microwave systems at the 28 gigaherz level. Mandl says there's room for more than one company to succeed, but that Teligent will stay competitive by relying on its own network, instead of leasing bits and pieces of the Bells' networks. That, he says, will save the company money.

Mandl also plans to remain focused on the fixed wireless market, where he says the economics are much more favorable than the mobile wireless market. Mobile wireless carriers must construct their entire network before they sign up customers, since users need to be able to travel about with their phones as soon as they sign up.

But fixed wireless carriers have the luxury of investing in infrastructure as they sign up customers, Mandl says. They can serve a small cluster of buildings without installing base stations all across town. An antenna and a base station are enough to connect the customer to the patchwork of the world's telephone networks. The construction costs will add up, though. The base stations are about $250,000, and antennas are about $15,000, installation included. Analysts estimate Teligent will spend $1 billion to construct its network.

A trial in Texas was successful, Mandl says. The company flew a group of stock analysts to Texas for a visit in late 1997, and the system was working fine despite a heavy rain. That's important, because fixed wireless systems are subject to inference in bad weather, some critics say.

Teligent plans to enter 74 markets by the year 2000. "We are going to grow revenue faster than any other company in the industry, and we are going to build network faster than it has ever been built before," Mandl vows.

David Friend and FaxNet
Telecom carrier as software company

The new telecommunications market reminds entrepreneur David Friend of the computer revolution of the 1980s. He understood from the beginning that the PC created huge opportunities for entrepreneurs. Multitudes of new computer users were entering the market with different needs, and they all needed new software programs to make their computers run according to their wishes. So Friend picked a niche and launched Pilot Software in 1982, developing databases and information systems for executives.

"I like being in places where the established order is being upset," says the 48-year-old Boston-based entrepreneur. "When I started in the software business it was going through wrenching change… I think out of turmoil comes opportunity… That is what you have in the phone business right now."

He sees two classes of companies emerging from the

chaos: (1) a handful of large carriers that own and operate telecom infrastructure, and (2) a new class of smaller companies like his latest venture, FaxNet, which ride the network with carefully targeted niche services. FaxNet is a telecommunications company just for fax users. Like his earlier venture, Pilot, it's essentially a software company. The difference is that Pilot wrote software that niche groups of customers ran on their PCs. FaxNet writes software that resides on the company's network, for use by targeted groups of telephone users. It reflects the unlimited opportunities created by the convergence of the telecommunications network and the computer.

"There is plenty of opportunity for new telecom companies," Friend says. "The question is how can software make the phone do something that is useful... You want to find some group of customers that have something in common and think, 'What can I do for these guys that is better than the one-size-fits-all service from the phone company,' which is what we did." The ideas seem to roll off Friend's tongue effortlessly: wireless faxes for people in cars, phones in airplanes, phone services for lawyers.

The tool of the trade: a programmable phone switch, such as FaxNet's $200,000 Summa Four. "We can make it do anything with the right software," Friend says.

His fascination with experimentation and change was sparked during childhood, although his early interests were in music, not business. Those first signs of invention were nurtured by his mother Miriam, a technical writer and amateur musician, and by his father Leo, a chemical engineer at W.W. Kellogg. He took piano lessons and developed an interest in composers, from Bach to Edgar Varese, an avantgarde composer who wrote for some of the first electronic musical instruments in the 1940s. As a high school student, he kept tabs on the electronic music laboratory at Columbia University.

Friend entered Yale University as a freshman in 1965, where his interests spanned the old and the new world. He helped found the Yale Bach Society, but he spent a lot of time in the electronic music studio as well. He graduated with a dual arts and engineering degree in 1969 and spent a year as a Sarnoff fellow at Princeton University, avoiding the draft and researching acoustic filters in a lab sponsored by RCA. His life changed forever later that year when Yale's alumni magazine wrote a cover story about his foray into the emerging field of electronic music. The story caught the attention of lawyer Lew Pollack, an older alumnus who was in the early stages of developing a new business to construct electronic instruments. He offered Friend a job.

"When I got into the synthesizer business, most of the music business was pianos and clarinets. I could see the electronic stuff was going to change all that," he recalled. "Electronic instruments were replacing acoustic instruments, or at least becoming their equals."

Selling to The Stones

Besides, Friend had decided that the academic pace didn't suit him. It was too slow. So he and his wife Margaret Shepherd loaded their 1969 Dodge Dart and headed north to Lexington, Massachusetts, where Pollack and his partner were developing electronic instruments with their company, ARP Instruments. The ARP synthesizer was a hit. Before long, Friend was selling instruments to Stevie Wonder, Les McCann, The Rolling Stones, The Who, Led Zeppelin, Todd Rundgren, Chick Corea, and Herbie Hancock. Friend was president of the company by age 25.

He ran ARP for ten years, but the seeds of his next venture were planted years before his tenure in the music business ended. ARP was among the first companies to use the computer to analyze demographic trends among its customers and markets. Other companies generally used their computers for clerical and accounting chores. Friend, a self-taught programmer, developed programs that plotted marketing data on charts, using an early color graphics terminal and a Digital Equipment Corp. computer.

CBS bought ARP in 1979. Friend took the sizable proceeds from that deal and started Computer Pictures the following year, capitalizing on the software he had written for ARP. He sold that business to Cullinet Corp., now known as Computer Associates, in 1983.

Friend struck up a partnership with a computer programmer named Jeff Flowers, and they decided to find a small but profitable niche in the burgeoning personal computer business. Microsoft and Apple Computer battled over operating systems, while IBM, Digital, and Wang pitted their mainframes against newer companies' PCs. Friend and Flowers launched Pilot Software in 1983. The idea was write PC programs that would help executives manage their information. The business was generating $40 million a year in revenue when he sold it to Dun & Bradstreet in 1994.

Friend was ready for a brief respite from the business world. He spent a semester at MIT, teaching and planning his next venture. Always searching for turmoil and change, he was drawn to telecommunications. He started FaxNet the following year. He wrote a business plan, conducted market research, and hired some staff to write the software, working with $4.3 million in venture funds. The software was written using a Compaq computer and a $200,000 programmable Summa Four switch. He also bought "industrial strength" Brook Trout fax modems capable of communicating with faxes in Asia and Europe, where technological standards are different. After six months of development, they were ready to start selling the service on a limited basis.

Never-Busy Fax

FaxNet's main product, known as Never-Busy Fax, makes sure that a fax always goes through. If the customer's fax line is busy, the network takes the call, stores the fax, and forwards it when the line is clear. Its primary market includes small to medium-size businesses that provide basic services such as law firms, printers, and flower shops. People who have a fax machine and a PC on the same phone line can surf the Web all day. Never-Busy Fax can be combined with long-distance and nearly a dozen enhanced services such as fax broadcasting, fax mail boxes, and fax on demand.

The company sold 1,300 accounts during the first week of business. It has a staff of ten in-house telemarketers who test sales scripts. Several outside telemarketing firms sell the service, too. The business is growing 10 to 15 percent a month, but Friend believes it will take two or three years to become profitable. The cost of acquiring customers is high, which makes it difficult to earn a profit and grow at the same time. "We can stop selling at any time, and when we do, it will be hugely profitable," Friend says. He plans to grow the company quickly in major markets, building revenue to several hundred million dollars a year. Next step: a public offering or a sale. Friend expects to build $1 billion in market capitalization within four years.

It's a high-margin business. The company was buying long-distance service for 8 cents to 9 cents a minute in 1996 and reselling it for 14.9 cents. The combination of long-distance and enhanced services produced revenue of 35 cents a minute.

Friend estimates that the $20 billion U.S. fax market will hit $34.5 billion in 1999. He's planning on taking just 0.3 percent, but that niche amounts to $100 million a year. Friend believes the fax market will only grow, even as newer and more exotic technologies arrive on the scene. He argues that the Internet will provide a new lower-cost transmission route for fax traffic, stimulating demand. "History has shown that lower communications costs are more than offset by increased usage and this explosion of usage has been good for new entrants," he says. And Friend says the fax machine is such a ubiquitous means of communication that there is little chance that e-mail traffic will replace it any time soon.

FaxNet faces little competition from the big carriers. In fact, the company signed agreements in 1997 with BellSouth and US West, which planned to resell FaxNet service in their local territories.

"We're just below their radar screen," Friend says. "The last thing they are worried about is the fax market. They are much more worried about deregulation, which is the heart of their business."

Jack Corn and Fax Source

Another telecom carrier as software company

Jack Corn just wasn't cut out for life on the family farm in Friend, Kansas. "I'd much rather be working on a computer in an air-conditioned office than on a tractor with the hot sun and dust hitting me," the 37-year-old founder of Fax Source explained. The businessman in him was apparent by the sixth grade, when he rose to a classic challenge laid down by his parents. Corn told his mother and father that he wanted to replace his heavy plastic eyeglasses with a pair of wire frames. They said that was fine, but that he'd have to come up with the $60 on his own. So Corn turned to the classified advertisements in the back of *Boys Life*, the scouting magazine, and landed a job selling metal Social Security cards. His first venture was a success. Corn retired from the metal Social Security card business with a new pair of glasses and $40 to spare.

Jack Corn

His drive deepened as he grew older. Junior year of high school: Jack Corn sells $1,600 worth of magazine subscriptions to raise money for the prom; wins water bed for efforts.

Kansas State University, 1978: Corn joins the marching band, which is selling chocolate-covered almonds to raise money for a trip to England. Vowing to sell more almonds than anyone else, Corn heads home for vacation with a strategy that targets Kansas alumni who own their own businesses. But he faces fierce competition from twin sisters, who appear to be selling the almonds in bulk through their father's business. Corn is upset, but he plays it cool and tells them, "You're way ahead; I'll never catch up."

Then he goes straight to the band office and checks out a massive amount of chocolate-covered almonds. "I was not going to be oversold," he says. He scoured the state selling candy to college alumni. He won the competition by selling $35,000 worth of candy.

He left school in 1982 with a degree in marketing and finance and visions of becoming a corporate CEO. Corn settled in Denver and landed a sales job at the Westin Hotel. He made sales manager within a few years, promoting the hotel for business meetings and conventions. By 1989, he was ready to go into business for himself.

Corn set up shop as a meeting planner, helping companies organize luxury trips as incentives for their top staff. The work kept him on the phone for much of the day, calling resorts and hotels for information about prices, rooms, business facilities, amenities, and transportation links. Most of the information arrived over the fax machine, a timesaving device that was just beginning to become standard equipment for large and small businesses alike. But it still took too much time locating the hotel staff responsible for sending him the information, and he had to rely on them to get the job done.

Fax Enters the Mainstream

As the months went by, Corn noticed that some of the hotels and resorts were making use of a new technology known as fax-on-demand. It allowed Corn to order information directly from a hotel's fax machine. The fax was connected to a voice-mail system and a computer. A recorded message presented a list of faxes that were available on demand. He selected the ones that he wanted by pressing buttons on his touch-tone phone. Then a computer faxed the information directly his way.

Corn was fascinated with the business potential of the new technology. The fax machine was entering the mainstream at a rapid pace, and fax-on-demand was bound to follow. His days planning corporate retreats were over. In 1989, he launched a new venture creating fax-on-demand systems for businesses in Denver. He called it Fax Source.

The first few months were rough. Corn financed the business with credit cards, running up as much as $50,000 in debt. The business began to turn the corner the following year, however, as yet another improvisation on the fax machine hit the street.

The new technology was known as fax broadcasting. It allowed the user to distribute a single fax to thousands of recipients at once. Corn began distributing newsletters and promotional faxes for the local hospitality and tourism industries, which he knew from his earlier career. He produced faxes announcing weekly ski conditions and deals on weekend getaways in Aspen. He produced a Vail Valley Guide and a Denver visitors guide, but growth was slow. Revenue for 1993 was only $23,000, and Corn lived on credit cards and faith. "I sincerely think something wonderful and big is about to happen to me and my family," he wrote in a journal entry dated May 8, 1993. "You see, I have been on my own for over a year now and as of today we have less than $700 in the bank." He admitted that it was "not quite the amount that one would get the feeling of something big is around the corner." Yet his intuition was correct.

Corn leased several T1 telephone lines, which have the data-carrying capacity of 24 traditional lines rolled into one. That allowed him to increase the number of faxes he could transmit at once. As Corn's fax broadcasting business grew, he noticed that Fax Source was getting quite a few telephone calls from recipients who didn't want to receive his transmissions and demanded to be taken off his distribution lists. Corn obliged them. He didn't stand to gain anything by transmitting information to people who didn't want to receive it. And besides, the Telecommunications

Protection Act made it illegal for a business to send a fax to another business or a consumer unless there was a business arrangement between them.

A Junk-Fax Antidote

This led, in 1996, to Corn unveiling a new product called Fax Me Not, a high-tech antidote to the junk fax. When Fax Me Not users receive an unwanted fax, they forward the fax and a special cover sheet to a computerized fax system at Corn's office in Denver. A computer device known as an optical character reader "reads" the cover letter, which includes the fax number that sent the unwanted fax in the first place. Fax Source's computer sends the offending party a fax message, saying its client wishes to be removed from the distribution list. About 85 percent of the problems are solved on the first try, and nearly all the rest are resolved on the second try. But just in case, the third cease-and-desist request carries a special note that legal action may be pending. Corn has a lawyer who is prepared to take people to court, but it hasn't come to that yet.

Fax Source had revenues of $300,000 in 1996 and expects to break a half million in the near future. Corn has eight people working for him, including a computer programmer. The company has several hundred clients, including a credit union executives society, a publishing company in San Francisco, and a firm that sells airfares to travel agents. The company drew 80 percent of its revenues from fax broadcasting in 1996.

Fax Source combines the fax broadcasting system with billing and marketing reports for Fax Source clients. It also records customer preferences, controlling whether or not its faxes should be distributed during peak or off-peak hours. Corn may license the technology to other fax broadcasting companies. It features a fax version of the reader response cards found in many magazines. They make it convenient for readers to request more information about products that are advertised in the publication. Readers can fill out the card and fax it to Fax Source, which uses its optical character reader to identify where the product information should be sent. It also faxes a message to the advertiser, announcing that a request for information has been received.

Fax Source has developed other niches, including Fax Me Not, all of which are based on the company's computer programming expertise. Corn heard that a competitor had laid off computer programmer Attila Safari, and Fax Source took him on for $125 an hour to help develop the new programs:

Regonline: This program allows people to register for conferences over the Internet. "Instead of one person entering data for 1,000 participants, you have 1,000 participants entering data for you," Corn says. The system accepts credit card payments, and it's combined with a telemarketing and fax broadcasting service that reminds prospective participants to register for the event.

Recall: Corn is developing a service bureau for conference calling companies that arrange teleconferences for their clients. It also allows people to replay audio conferences that are stored on the Web.

Real estate lead line: Fax Source is also offering a service that builds Web sites for the real estate industry. People who visit the sites can also request additional information be faxed to them.

Corn is also contemplating the acquisition of a small fax broadcasting company that has failed to make a profit. "With our technology, we can make it very profitable," he says.

"There is so much to do," Corn says. "But we are really tying to hone in on niches. We are not trying to do everything for everyone."

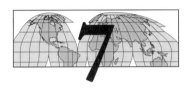

Bernie Bossard, Shant Hovnanian, and CellularVision

High-speed wireless access into the home and office

Electrical engineer Bernie Bossard stumbled across a virtually unused portion of the microwave spectrum during his research in the 1980s. The super-high-frequency radio spectrum, unknown to all but a handful of Defense Department researchers, was like a vast swath of undeveloped beachfront property. Free from the interference issues that plague the crowded lower reaches of the radio band, the higher frequencies offer enough space to carry live two-way video as well as voice. The only problem was that the spectrum shared a beach's vulnerability to bad weather. Signals at this extreme end of the radio band tend to break up in storms. Bossard, a veteran of the Patriot missile program, decided in 1986 that he was going to solve that problem.

"The key was to put lots of signals together without causing distortion," said Bossard, a tousle-haired, self-effacing professorial sort. He decided to broadcast 28 gigaherz signals from a main transmitter, or head end, to antennas that covered small geographic areas known as cells. At three miles in diameter, the cells were small enough to control distortion. He used repeaters to boost the signal and beam it into pockets that were out of the main antenna's line-of-sight. He called the technique Local Multipoint Distribution System (LMDS).

Bossard was impressed with the design: It eliminated the need for a direct line of sight between transmitter and receiver, solving a problem that has plagued many satellite and land-based transmission systems. It eliminated the capacity constraints of other radio-based systems, too, creating a possible alternative to cable TV operators and phone companies alike.

Bossard sought help from the venture-capital community in Boston, but he had trouble raising funds because he didn't yet have a patent for the technology. But a sympathizer directed him to V.S. Hovnanian Group, part of the Hovnanian home-building empire in New Jersey. Vahak Hovnanian and son Shant provided their own cable TV systems at their developments. They found the systems expensive and difficult to maintain, and they were receptive to Bossard's wireless alternative. It was the beginning of an 11-year battle to launch a new industry.

They created CellularVision to bring the idea to life, with Shant Hovnanian as CEO and Bossard as chief technical officer. They tested the system at Hovnanian developments in Asbury Park and Freehold, New Jersey, between 1986 and 1988. They won a patent for the technology in 1988 and applied for a license to provide LMDS service in the New York area. The group won a license from the Federal Communications Commission in 1991 after three years of opposition from local phone companies and satellite services. CellularVision raised $43 million in financing from

Bell Atlantic, Philips Electronics, and J.P. Morgan in 1993.

The emergence of the World Wide Web in 1995 created yet another use for the system. CellularVision is offering phone service, television, and high-speed Internet access in parts of New York, and it was preparing to offer an even higher-speed digital service as 1997 drew to a close. It is also suited for live two-way videoconferencing. The analog system allows users to download files from the Internet at speeds of about 550 kilobits a second, which is about ten times as fast as a 56 kilobit a second modem. A new digital system promises speeds of 35 to 58 megabits a second. A high-speed T1 phone line carries only 1.54 megabits a second.

After years of delay, the FCC was scheduled to auction licenses covering the rest of the United States in February 1998, providing entrepreneurs who want to compete in the phone, television, or data markets with an alternative technology. It would be the largest auction of spectrum in history. "I expect everyone to show up. This is such a large auction of capacity, it can't be ignored," Hovnanian says. "You really have the ability to compete with everybody." Hovnanian and Bossard are also partners in CT&T, a privately held company that licenses LMDS technology around the world. Canada, Russia, Panama, and the Philippines are introducing the technology in their markets.

CellularVision of New York is operating in sections of Manhattan and Brooklyn. It offers residential customers a basic package of 31 television stations for about $20 a month. Business services in Manhattan and Brooklyn include broadcasts of Bloomberg Information TV. CellularVision's 12,000 customers receive the service via six-inch-square antennas fixed to their window or roof.

The capital markets, deeply skeptical of other wireless technologies, have shown little interest so far. CellularVision held an initial public offering in February 1997, selling shares of its stock at $15 each. The price sunk to $10 later in the year. Wall Street soured on nearly all kinds of wireless companies. Perhaps the acronym LMDS was just too similar to MMDS (Multi-Channel Multi-Point Distribution Service). Bell Atlantic had once planned to deploy MMDS, which operates at a lower frequency and a lower bandwidth than LMDS, as a television service in the Northeast, but it broke off its plans.

Hovnanian says the major advantages of LMDS are its enormous capacity, comparable to fiber-optic cable, and its favorable economics. CellularVision says it costs about $370 to connect a customer to the network, compared to more than $1,000 for cable TV or fiber optic-cable connections. The challenge, of course, is proving that the technology will live up to expectations during large-scale deployment in the market.

Bossard won't speculate about the financial future of CellularVision or LMDS. "I'm not a fortune-teller. We'll see what happens," he says. But he is already enjoying the satisfaction of watching his ideas come to life. "It's great to see an industry forming around an idea. I'm not an egomaniac. It's just nice to see."

Dwight Ryan and A/E/C Express

*Creating a niche
in the satellite market*

Dietzgen Corp. was looking for ways to expand its core businesses, which supplies paper and digital-imaging products to the architectural, engineering, and construction market. It noticed that computers were rapidly replacing traditional drawing techniques, but that delivery of these documents was still done by hand. Dietzgen decided that it was going to take the industry to the next stage of the digital revolution: the network stage. It launched A/E/C Express to deliver digital documents over a high-speed satellite network provides same-day delivery for the price of overnight delivery by human courier.

A/E/C Express, as the service is known, began operating in late 1997, allowing builders and architects to send files anywhere in the United States or Canada in four hours. The company says its system is 100 times faster than the high-speed phone lines known as Integrated Services Digital Network. Those ISDN lines transmit 128 kilobits a second. A/E/C can transmit a typical five megabit blueprint file from Chicago to San Francisco in five minutes. It's printed out at a local point on the satellite network and delivered by hand to the company that ordered the document.

A/E/C had installed its hardware and software systems at about 50 architectural, engineering, and construction firms around the country as 1997 ended. Clients have been offered two-year licenses for about $1,500 a month, a flat fee that's recovered as long as they send or receive six files a day. It's building on the $500,000 to $1 million investment these companies have already made in digital-imaging technology.

Dietzgen, which is owned by the Weyerhaeuser family, says U.S. architectural, engineering, and construction firms spend $500 million a year to transmit 15 million documents via overnight delivery service. A/E/C CEO Dwight Ryan says the company can take at least $50 million of that U.S. market in the near term. It also plans to enter the $1.5 billion global market, too. "We're faster and we charge the same price," says Ryan, a former president of Xerox's North American sales and service group.

This is just one example of how a small to medium-size business can tap the quickly growing satellite market. It also reflects how companies can develop a niche in telecommunications by building on what they already know, tapping their knowledge of a particular market and their relationships with customers.

Opportunities for satellite transmission are growing. Prices will fall as new generations of devices are launched into space. A/E/C is paying $59,000 a month to lease part of the capacity of a satellite that orbits 23,000 miles above the earth. Its clients connect to the network using Very Small Aperture Terminals (VSATs) that are less than six feet in diameter.

New options are on the way, including low-orbit satellites that operate 400 to 1,000 miles above the earth, and middle-orbit satellites that operate about 6,000 miles up. Low-orbit satellites can operate with smaller, lighter, lower-powered devices, and could push satellite technology into a broader market. High-profile low-earth satellite ventures include Iridium, a venture of Motorola and other big companies, which plans to offer global phone service in 1998. Bill Gates and Craig McCaw plan to create an "Internet in the Sky" with their Teledesic venture, which is slated for operations in 2002.

The profusion of satellite capacity will create new opportunities for carriers such as A/E/C, which lease use of the infrastructure and provide highly targeted niche services. A/E/C itself expects to expand its service into new markets. "Satellites can transmit court records, large medical files, and libraries of data," Ryan says. Satellites can transmit dailies for the motion picture industry. It has disaster-relief applications, too. It was merely coincidental that an architect was nearby to help locate victims trapped by the Oklahoma City bombing, Ryan says. A disaster relief service could transmit blueprints when the architect isn't on hand.

Robert Annunziata and Teleport Communications

Executing strategy in a chaotic market

All telecommunications companies talk about the importance of execution, or carrying out their grand strategies in the day-to-day world of business. Few can match the record of Teleport Communications Group (TCG).

This competitive local exchange carrier, which competes with the regional Bells for big corporate accounts, impresses Wall Street analysts with its mastery of the details. "Especially noteworthy during the quarter was the company's ability to provision 20 percent of the lines added in the quarter within one hour," Merrill Lynch analyst Dan Reingold wrote in a November 1997 report. "That compares quite favorably versus the 30–45 day turnaround typically seen in the (competitive local exchange carrier) industry."

That's the benefit of experience. Teleport Communications is the oldest competitive local exchange carrier in the business. Financed by Merrill Lynch (which has since sold the business) and run by an AT&T veteran named Robert Annunziata, Teleport has been offering local phone service to big corporations since 1983. It has become one of the hottest companies in the industry. Expectations for earnings, which are expected to start flowing in 2001, are running high. The company is the subject of perennial takeover talk on Wall Street, where its stock was near an all-time high as 1997 ended. At 49, Annunziata is widely regarded as one of the industry's top chief executives, thanks to his record of getting things done.

"I think the two most important things in running a business are information systems and people," he says. Annunziata remembers the days in the mid-1980s when it took big corporations a year to get a high-speed T1 phone line from one of the big phone companies. Teleport was able to provision a new line in a week or two. Annunziata determined several years ago that even a week wasn't fast enough. He sat down with his information services department and came up with a plan.

The idea was to eliminate the need for people to re-enter the same data in the system over and over by hand. It's a problem that has characterized phone companies for decades. Their systems often predated the computer itself, and the conversion to a fully digital environment was difficult and slow. Teleport decided to automate its own operations as much as possible. After a customer representative in Denver receives a new order over the phone, a message is automatically sent to the customer premises department to make sure there's enough capacity on the network to absorb the new business. The operations department is told to provide equipment at the customer's office. The accounting departments and network monitoring center are notified as well.

"It cross-connects without human interaction," Annunziata says. That helps the company fulfill an order for a new customer in a day or two. An existing customer can receive a new service in a matter of hours.

Internal systems function with similar efficiency. Any of the company's officers can request capital for a project, and when Annunziata signs off on the request, the others are notified. Of course, officers are required to make their capital investments pay off. The internal financial systems also allow Annunziata to monitor every action in the company from his desktop.

The company espouses a doctrine of continuous improvement and invests heavily in its people, who visit a corporate training facility in New Jersey 10 or 15 days a year. It takes care of its people with a range of benefits that are geared to their needs at various stages of life. The company has dropped the term "department of human resources" and created a People Services Department that reports directly to Annunziata. "Life-cycle benefits and information systems are there to help people do their jobs better," Annunziata says.

The company has grown under his watch. Today, Teleport is by far the largest of the competitive local exchange carriers, with 8,700 miles of fiber-optic cable and a presence in 65 markets around the country. Teleport had more than 200,000 local phone lines under its control in mid-1997, nearly five times as many as number two Brooks Fiber, which was being acquired by WorldCom as 1997 drew to a close.

Teleport has half a billion dollars in annual revenue, and investors are looking forward to its first net profits, which are expected in 2001. A perennial subject of takeover speculation on Wall Street, the company's shares were trading near an all-time high in late 1997 as industrywide consolidation focused attention on the stock. With revenues expected to hit $8 billion by 2007, Teleport could emerge as one of the new giants of the telecommunications industry, if another player doesn't buy it first. "If someone comes along with an appropriate price, we will do what is best for our shareholders," Annunziata says.

Teleport's early start shaped its strategy. "As a pioneer, TCG had no one to rely on but itself," analyst Bruce Roberts of SBC Warburg Dillon Reed wrote in September 1997. "It couldn't count on the (incumbent local exchange carriers) to share or lease facilities; so from the outset TCG became a 100 percent facilities-based provider, which means that it built its own local fiber loops."

Its purchase of Eastern Telelogic fills out a footprint from New Hampshire to Virginia. It also had to pursue large companies in big markets such as New York, where the company could tie lots of big customers to a single line, making the most of its investment. But Teleport is using its original niche to expand into new markets such as medium-size and small businesses.

Teleport is growing by acquisition. It bought BizTel, allowing it to offer high-speed wireless services in 200 markets. It also outbid Tel-Save Holdings for ACC Corp., a long-distance carrier. It has even entered the pay phone business, signing up customers such as Harvard University. Its acquisition of CERFnet put Teleport in the Internet-access business, too.

"We are going to keep growing. You will find Teleport a major player in this industry," Annunziata says.

Tom Brandenburg and USN Communications

Pioneering local resale in the business market

Venturing wholeheartedly into the most maligned sector of the telecommunications business, USN Communications is staking its future on the resale of local phone service. Purchasing local phone service at wholesale rates from Ameritech and Bell Atlantic, USN is venturing into territory that bigger carriers have all but abandoned.

AT&T stopped marketing its local resale business in late 1997, less than one year after it began. AT&T, MCI, and Sprint have complained bitterly that government-set prices don't allow them to make a profit and that the country's dominant local phone companies exploit their control of customer records, phone numbers, and physical networks to keep competitors at bay. Nearly every major new entrant in the local telecommunications sector has decided to invest billions of dollars in network construction, rather than

Tom Brandenburg

resell the service of the existing carriers.

USN founder Tom Brandenburg admits that it's a difficult business. But he says USN has two huge advantages: an extremely early entrance into the market and a fierce determination to make the business work. It didn't have anything else to fall back upon if the resale strategy failed. It may be too late to duplicate USN's strategy, since it depended on quick timing. But USN is an important example of how companies can gain crucial advantage by getting to market first.

Brandenburg was one of the original investors in long-distance upstart LCI in 1983. He could have retired to his farm in the Hamptons for the rest of his life, but the start of a second family rekindled his energy. The family moved to Chicago in 1993, and Brandenburg started exploring ideas for a new business. He was interested in selling enhanced telecommunications services, the kinds of features that aren't included in a regular monthly local bill. Brandenburg, who had also spent time on Wall Street, was able to raise an initial $1 million from a group of private investors. He also attracted $100 million in venture capital from CIBC Wood Gundy, Hancock Venture Partners, and Chase Capital Partners. He hired an attorney named Ron Gavillet, who was ready to try something new after working as a lawyer at Skadden Arps and MCI. Brandenburg and Gavillet set up shop in a former dentist's office in Chicago, complete with a sliding glass window separating the front office from the waiting room.

Since deregulation had been creating new choices for business customers since the late 1980s, Brandenburg was convinced that the local phone market was a bigger opportunity than long-distance. "The huge opportunity was always on the local beachhead," says Brandenburg, now 61. "The suppressed demand in what was always the larger market was just beginning to grow. And now we have the increasing growth of data."

The question was how to tap that opportunity. Brandenburg's first impulse was to build his own local networks, just as MFS, Teleport, and other competitive local exchange carriers had. "We started down the road to being a facilities-based carrier, but it didn't take long to grow great respect for the telephone infrastructure constructed over the last 100 years for billions of dollars, and the high quality delivered with it." USN abandoned any plans to rebuild the local phone network, refocusing its energy on repacking and re-marketing existing services in new ways. The company also targeted a sector of the market that hadn't received much attention: small and medium-size businesses.

Brandenburg said that the established local phone companies were steeped in engineering experience and had constructed a great network, but they weren't necessarily known for their marketing and customer service. And the regional Bells were barred from entering the long-distance market. He envisioned USN as an integrator of local, long-distance, data, and enhanced services such as voice-mail, combined on a single bill, sold face to face by the sales force and serviced through a single point of contact with the customer. Reselling the Bell networks would also allow USN to share their ubiquitous presence, something that the facilities-based competitors couldn't easily achieve.

Timing and 'Co-opetition'

The challenge was to convince the regional Bell carriers to share their networks on terms that were economically favorable to both parties. USN proposed the idea of *co-opetition*. He presented USN as a rival, to be sure, but one that would double as a major customer, keeping traffic on Bell networks amid new competition from upstarts with independent new networks. "It was a tough sale," Brandenburg recalls. But the company managed to strike a ten-year resale agreement with Ameritech in November 1995, the first of its kind in the nation. It was signed four months before the Telecommunications Act of 1996 was even enacted, giving USN a head start of a year or more on other local resellers.

If USN had waited another year to negotiate its resale agreements, as other carriers did, it would have been forced to live with the same government-mandated margins in the 20 to 25 percent range. It would have had to stand in line at the negotiating table behind dozens of other companies, and its talks would been conducted amid the lawsuits and rhetorical wars that have overshadowed local resale since mid-1996.

USN's head start allowed it to negotiate a better deal and to establish a relationship with Ameritech and Nynex, which is now part of Bell Atlantic. Its resale agreement includes a 20 percent discount off the retail price for basic local service, but its discounts on enhanced services are in the 45 to 50 percent range. "If you blend it all together, the discount is about 30 percent," Brandenburg says.

USN agreed to buy at least 150,000 phone lines in Chicago, 100,000 in Michigan, and 100,000 in New York, but the company has several years to meet its commitments. "We took a risk in the negotiations in terms of the volume agreements that deliver us margins over-and-above the resale rates that AT&T and MCI are complaining about," Brandenburg says.

USN has since raised an additional $200 million from high-yield debt investors, and it has filed to issue $80 million worth of stock. The company has been operating since November 1996 in Chicago. Its "USNfreedom" brand offers services geared toward business: bills that feature accounting codes, so that calls can be associated with particular projects; authorization codes that limit use of the network to employees; and advanced routing features for its customers' sales and customer service departments. Revenue from these enhanced services has been growing about 25 percent a year on an industrywide basis, far surpassing the single-digit growth rates that have characterized basic phone service for generations. The company also spent its first two years making sure the computer and physical connections between USN and Ameritech and Bell Atlantic were working properly. These systems, which must quickly transfer a customer from one carrier to another, are a crucial component of a competitive market. They have been the source of bitter complaints by AT&T and MCI. "It's easy to find flaws," Brandenburg says, "but we actually had incentive to make it work."

It will be some time before the results of USN's experiment are known. "We're not profitable yet; we're a growth company," Brandenburg says. But he's confident it will be. "We saw a window of opportunity and knew we could make the business grow while the big carriers were fighting in court and arguing and litigating and complaining."

Vern Kennedy and Community Telephone

Local resale in the residential market

The Telecommunications Act of 1996 requires the nation's local phone monopolies to make their networks available to competitors. The law requires them to provide computer connections between networks, so that newcomers will have access to lists of customer names, phone numbers, and maintenance records. It also instructs regulators to set wholesale prices for the market.

Few aspects of the Telecommunications Act have received so much criticism. Competitors say that the computer connections are unworkable and that the prices don't create enough of a margin to make a profit. AT&T stopped marketing nearly all of its local resale operations at the end of 1997, making just a few exceptions for testing purposes. AT&T and MCI say local carriers are to blame, although the big local phone companies say the long-distance carriers

Vern Kennedy

really don't want to compete.

As the giants of the telecommunications industry wage rhetorical and legal battle over the terms of competition, at least one small company is quietly trying to make a living at resale. Operating in an old Contadina ketchup factory in the heart of Queens, New York, Community Telephone is trying to do the impossible: resell the services of the dominant local phone company under its own brand name and make a profit.

"I saw a tremendous opportunity," says Vern Kennedy, Community's 31-year-old CEO. "This market is going to break wide open… and I thought I was uniquely qualified to be one of the first folks out there." Armed with a bachelor's degree in electrical engineering from Princeton University and an MBA from New York University, Kennedy rose through the ranks of Nynex over the course of eight years. His last position was director of operations on Long Island, where he supervised 500 people and had profit and loss responsibility.

Community took the first residential customer from Nynex (now Bell Atlantic) in New York State on October 8, 1996. It has signed up 5,000 residential and business customers since then. That's a tiny fraction of Bell Atlantic's phone lines, but Kennedy says the company is just getting started.

Most states require dominant local phone companies to offer competitors a discount of 20 percent to 25 percent off retail rates. "Clearly, the wholesale discounts are too low relative to what the costs are," Kennedy says. And he can't understand why Bell Atlantic can offer a 19 percent discount in New York and a 29 percent discount in Massachusetts. "Do they have that many more costs in Massachusetts?" he wonders. An entrepreneur could probably create a going concern by focusing just on local resale, but it's not an exciting opportunity unto itself.

The money comes from combining local service with other products such as long-distance, wireless, Internet access, and high-speed data services such as T1 and frame relay, says Kennedy. Community offers all five. "You have fixed costs of customer acquisition. You have fixed costs of billing and customer service. And now you take the margins from long-distance, cellular, data, calling cards, and, in some places, video resale. You layer them on top of local and now you are starting to talk about a pretty attractive financial package," he says.

Kennedy expects margins in local resale itself to improve, making the financial package even more lucrative. As new carriers build physical networks that compete with the Bells, networks will compete for the business of resellers. "We'll see (wholesale) prices drop pretty dramatically," he says. Until then, Kennedy is grappling with all the challenges of a start-up telecom carrier. He raised $2 million in start-up funds from a network of two dozen friends and family. He assembled a young team of managers. Tracy Korman, 34, a former Booz Allen & Hamilton consultant, signed on as vice president of sales and marketing. T.J. Anderson, 31, a former media and telecom banker, came aboard as chief financial officer.

They have identified what they believe are numerous under-served markets:

⊡ Small to medium-size businesses that spend $500 to $5,000 a month on telecommunications. "We're looking for the kind of business where the owner is also the CEO and the telecom guy," Kennedy says.

⊡ Middle-income residential customers in Brooklyn, the Bronx, and Queens, where the company's flyers can be spotted on lampposts. It also markets from a calling center at headquarters.

⊡ Small office-home office (SOHO) customers.

⊡ Immigrants who often spend a lot of money calling abroad and are "underwhelmed" with their choices.

Community says its offers consumers a 10 percent discount on Bell Atlantic prices; businesses get 5 percent off. It also invested in development of its own billing system, reflecting a priority on customer service.

With a staff of 35, the company is boosting its revenues by 10 percent to 20 percent a month. "We could break even very quickly if we wanted to," Kennedy says. "A lot of our profit and loss is driven by sales and marketing. To the extent we slow those down, we break even. But we see a period of opportunity here for a number of years, and we'll be showing losses for that entire period."

Patrick Palmer and Freefone

The anti-pay phone

They look like pay phones, but without the coin slots. Mounted inside three-foot-tall shelters that hang from the walls of skating rinks, bowling alleys, and doctors' offices in Houston, Patrick Palmer's phones are nearly indistinguishable from millions of other phones in public places. But these phones are free for use.

Each phone booth is plastered with nine advertisements for local businesses. The phones dispense free three-minute local calls, luring people into the booths, where they are exposed to the ads. "The phone is just a vehicle to sell the advertising," says Palmer, the president of Freefone.

"I'm just the type of person who has a difficult time working within a structure, per se, other than my own," says Palmer, 38, a longtime entrepreneur. The dentist's son graduated from the University of Texas in 1982 with a degree in biology, but he went into business instead of science. Palmer has run a computer-hardware business, traded oil and sold cars over the years, but it appears Freefone may be the opportunity he has been hoping to find. After four years of development, the business appears to be catching hold. He installed 15 phones in Houston as of late 1997, and was selling franchises for other territories such as San Antonio, Austin, Dallas, and Denver. He planned to advertise franchises for territories across the United States in 1998. "The public loves it," he says. They aren't all-purpose phones, though. They can't be used for any sort of long-distance call, including toll-free calls, and they don't provide access to directory services. Freefone can be used to place calls to 911, though.

Palmer was originally looking for a way to sell low-cost advertising. He wanted to sell ads for street maps, but the idea had already been taken. Then he thought of Freefone. He worked with several vendors to develop the steel phones, which he assembles in a warehouse. He sells them for $3,000 at the franchise level and installation costs run $250. The phone bills run up to $60 a month per phone. Generating $8,100 a year in advertising revenue, Palmer says the phones achieved a 100 percent return during the first year. "The second year, the phone is paid for," he says. "There is nothing like it out there in terms of return on investment."

It's one of several free calling services that have cropped up around the world. Gratistelefon of Sweden allows people to make free phone calls from home in exchange for listening to advertisements over the phone. Primosat of Italy offers a similar service.

So far, free phone services are supported by advertising. But some analysts believe all voice calls may be free one day, developing into a perk that carriers offer customers who buy advanced data and video services. "The real value of phone service will be about 1 cent a month," says Francis McInerney, of North River Ventures, the telecommunications investment firm. "What will be worth something is broadband services to the home."

Daniel Borislow and Tel-Save

Marketing telecommunications over the Web

Marketing became a huge expense for long-distance companies after the breakup of AT&T and the onset of competition. The battle for customers was waged on prime-time network television with armies of celebrities hawking AT&T, Sprint, and MCI. AT&T's marketing expenses peaked at $1 billion in the mid-1990s, and The Yankee Group still estimates them at $800 million a year. Marketing is a major expense for smaller carriers, too. Nearly one-quarter of the country's resellers spend more than 17 percent of their revenue on sales and marketing.

The industry has experimented with several successful efforts to cut these costs. A new generation of smaller companies, such as Excel, pared expenses by skipping the television commercials and recruiting ordinary people to sell the service directly to their friends, family, and acquaintances. That led big companies such as AT&T to break the expensive habit of luring new customers with $100 checks.

The most important change in telecom marketing, however, may have occurred in March 1997. That's when a relatively small long-distance carrier known as Tel-Save struck a marketing agreement with America Online, shifting marketing, billing, and customer service into cyberspace. More than a mere cost-cutting effort, the agreement has the potential to create a new economic model for the telecommunications industry.

Tel-Save was already a success story when it struck the deal with AOL. The company has been a low-cost provider since it was launched in 1989, thanks to founder and CEO Daniel Borislow's practical experience in the construction industry and his obsession with technology.

"I'm a technology freak. I always made my money by being more efficient than everyone else," says the 36-year-old CEO. He was different than his father, a psychologist, and his brothers, a doctor and a member of the investment industry. He describes himself as an ultra-competitive person who has never worked for anyone else. "I have two big interests in life. One is making money. The other is spending it," says Borislow, who owns several horses.

He spent most of his time at Widener University playing soccer, and left without a degree to start a construction company. Borislow says he built 30 percent of the cable television systems in Philadelphia. He intended to use his construction experience and build new local phone networks that would compete in the business market with the local phone monopolies, but he took a detour into long-distance instead.

Tel-Save bought its long-distance service exclusively from AT&T, eventually becoming one of the giant carrier's largest customers. If AT&T retail customers were paying 25 cents a minute, Tel-Save would pay 9 cents and resell it to other carriers for 12 cents. Those carriers might sell the service to the public at 20 cents a minute.

Tel-Save kept its costs low. It hired AT&T to do its billing. And it developed efficient operating systems for filling customer orders and providing customer service. Special charges aside, the company has been profitable since the end of its first year of operations, Borislow says. He poured those profits back into the company in 1995, investing in five AT&T switches that gave Tel-Save more control over its operations and improved its operating margins.

The company went public at the end of 1995, and Wall Street loved it. The shares appreciated 300 percent between the December 1995 public offering and the fall of 1997. They rose 200 percent in 1996, the best performance in the U.S. telecommunications sector. Institutional investors include GT Global, Fidelity, MFS Investment Co., and Putnam. The company has raised more than $600 million in the last two years.

A Marketing Deal With AOL

As 1997 drew to a close, Borislow was completing an acquisition of Shared Technologies, a local phone carrier. He had launched a bid for ACC, a long-distance carrier with global reach. And perhaps most important of all, he was executing a breakthrough marketing agreement to sell phone service over America Online. "Life changes with the AOL deal," Borislow says.

Borislow approached the leading online service in early 1997 as it was suffering through the worst time in its history. The network was growing at breakneck speed. AOL was signing up customers as fast as it could and giving them unlimited access for $19.95 a month. The network couldn't handle the new traffic and it crashed again and again, raising the blood pressure of consumers and even government officials. The stock was in a deep slump.

Tel-Save proposed that the companies strike a partnership to sell long-distance service online, creating a new brand name of AOL Long Distance. AOL would get a share of the profits, creating a valuable new source of cash for the rapidly expanding network, and a perk that would help retain customers. Tel-Save benefitted by becoming the first long-distance carrier to shift its sales and service to the Web. The agreement was designed to benefit both companies and their customers:

Payment: It's generally impossible for phone companies to get their customers to pay by credit card. Tel-Save overcomes this obstacle by adding long-distance service onto the credit-card bills of AOL's on-line customers. This allows Tel-Save to receive payments much more quickly than other phone companies do, which generally suffer through billing cycles of two months. It also eliminates the problem of bad debt. Tel-Save also saves the cost of preparing a bill, which is about $1.50 a month for each customer, and the cost of cashing their checks, which is about 35 cents each.

Billing: Consumers get the convenience of combining a variety of services on a single bill, and nearly instantaneous access to their calling records. Tel-Save constructed its own billing system. Calls appear on their on-line bill 15 minutes after they are made. The bill can also be customized to suit customers' needs. And they get a flat rate of 9 cents a minute for long-distance calls any time of day or night, Borislow says.

Marketing costs: Tel-Save slashed marketing costs. AOL contributed $100 million worth of on-line advertisements over the three-year life of the agreement, giving Tel-Save free access to a medium that other carriers pay dearly to use. The advertisements also plug Tel-Save into the most profitable part of the residential market: AOL customers have an average income of about $75,000 a year and make lots of long-distance calls. The service will also be featured in AOL's list of membership perks.

The new service will help Tel-Save battle the industry-wide problem of churn, the term for customers who switch from one carrier to another. The root of the problem is that few carriers offer their customers a service that can't be duplicated by competitors. Borislow says Tel-Save's 9-cent-a-minute rate resists churn because the competition can't match its low-cost, Web-based operating structure. "We should be able to keep our customers," Borislow says. AT&T WorldNet, Microsoft Network, and other on-line services may offer similar long-distance plans, but they can't match the scale of AOL, which has 50 percent of the on-line market.

The AOL deal includes long-distance service, but Tel-Save is taking other steps to enter the local market and the international long-distance market. It tried to acquire ACC Corp. and Shared Technologies, which would have expanded its networks around the country and the world. Those deals fell through, however.

Borislow envisions several internal avenues of growth for Tel-Save, including signing up a higher percentage of the tenants in the buildings it already serves and expanding its network into new markets such as residential apartment buildings and colleges and universities. "They are great markets. They aggregate a lot of customers in a small area and that is how you make money in the CLEC (competitive local exchange carrier) market," he says.

Borislow is drawing on his experience in cable TV construction to keep the build-out cost of the expansion well below the industry average. Industry experts say it generally costs well over $1,000 a customer to construct a local network. Borislow says he can hook them up for $200 each by using a combination of Bell transmission lines and his own compression equipment.

To provide local service to a large apartment building, for example, Borislow will begin with a pair of standard copper phone wires that he leases from the neighborhood's dominant carrier. Then he'll convert the lines into a T1 line, the equivalent of 24 regular lines, using his own compression equipment. That's enough capacity to serve

150 customers in a building, or a neighborhood, because only one in six customers will use the phone at any given time. Each line will produce an estimated $70 a month in revenue, for a total of $10,500.

By using his own compression equipment, Borislow can boost the phone lines for Internet traffic. Most people who buy 56-kilobit-per-second modems are unable to take advantage of the advertised speed, because the phone lines can only handle speeds in the 30-kilobit-per-second range. Newer technology will allow customers to take advantage of their 56 kilobit modems.

Laura Scher and Working Assets

Affinity marketing

Working Assets and AT&T are different political animals. AT&T canceled its support of Planned Parenthood years ago, saying it had no business taking a stand in the debate over birth control or abortion. Working Assets, however, invites its customers to contribute 1 percent or more of their phone bills every month to Planned Parenthood and many other liberal causes. It invites its customers to make free phone calls to Washington to lobby for human rights, the environment, and economic and social justice.

AT&T, the most widely held stock in the United States, is legally bound to put the interests of its shareholders first. Laura Scher, the 38-year-old CEO of privately held Working Assets, says making money is simply an end to a higher mission. She shunned the high salaries of Wall Street and big corporations, saying that she had no interest in making enormous amounts of cash.

Laura Scher

AT&T's marketing tactics might not appear to have much in common with the activism of Working Assets, but beneath their differences, these companies share an increasingly common approach to business. Many of the ideas about marketing that AT&T and other carriers, big and small, have embraced during the late 1990s were pioneered by Working Assets in the late 1980s. It has established a deep rapport with its customers, one based on shared values and a thorough knowledge of one another.

"All entrepreneurs have a sort of vision," Scher says. "The vision of Working Assets was to create products so that people could spend their money in a socially responsible fashion, to have a values-driven company." The daughter of a chemical company owner in New Jersey, Scher grew up immersed in political activism and business. She graduated at the top of her class at Harvard Business School, and became CEO of Working Assets Funding Service in 1985 at the behest of founder Peter Barnes.

Big carriers such as AT&T are recreating themselves around the ideas of customer focus, tight market segmentation, and helping customers in their everyday lives. AT&T declared in 1997 that its new mission was no less than the improvement of its customers' lives. On a tactical level, carriers are trying to establish intimate relationships with their customers by elevating the monthly bill from the status of payment mechanism to that of marketing tool.

Working Assets Funding was an offshoot of the Working Assets Money Market Fund. It began life as a credit card company and moved into the long-distance phone business. Customers can donate 1 percent of their bill to designated causes, or they can round their bill up to the next $5 or $10 increment and donate the difference. Revenues have grown from $2 million in 1991 to about $100 million. Working Assets is expanding into the deregulated power market, too.

Working Assets can be viewed as a triumph of affinity marketing, and to that extent it is a model for the industry. Most companies segment their market in traditional economic terms. They pursue companies of a particular size, or households with a certain income or certain spending habits. Working Assets caters to a market that has an affinity for certain political ideas. It's a strong bond, too. Its customers are unlikely to switch to another carrier that comes along with a slightly cheaper price for long-distance service.

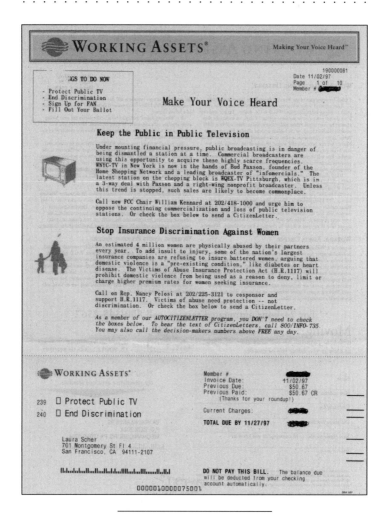

Sample Bill from Working Assets

"Our mailings are targeted more toward psychographic characteristics than demographic predilections," Scher says. The company rents mailing lists from direct-mail consulting firms that broker the names of American consumers. Then it sorts through the list for prospective customers that meet its criteria. Working Assets customers tend to read books more often than they watch TV. Thirty percent have gone to graduate school. Many of them live on the East

Coast or West Coast, and they tend to recycle their trash and vote. Scher attributes the company's swift growth to these techniques. "That's how we grew the business," she says.

Gail McGovern, AT&T's executive vice president for consumer markets, used that same word—*psychographics*—as she outlined the company's market strategy to analysts in March 1997. The two companies are pursuing different targets, but the method is the same. AT&T introduced two new "bundles" of service based on this methodology in November 1997. "That's what's going on in the '90s—figuring out peoples' behavior," Scher says.

Having identified a new customer, the next step is to create a lasting bond that competitors can't break. Working Assets entered the long-distance business as a sales agent for Sprint in 1988. It became a reseller in 1991 so it could take control of its billing." We really built this sophisticated information system," Scher says, "It's more than a bill."

The "bill" features four components:

Free Calls, Free Speech: Each bill features a current issue, and lists names and numbers of political and business leaders with influence over the debate. Customers can make two free calls a day to specific decision-makers.

CitizenLetters: Customers can also send decision-makers letters written by Working Assets. Its issues for January and February 1997 included the federal budget, family planning, the use of chlorine to whiten paper, and chemical weapons.

Eye on Congress: News of Capitol Hill, such as issues before Congress of interest to customers.

Recycled media: The bill itself is printed on 100 percent recycled paper and printed with soy-based ink. The company also plants 17 trees for every ton of paper that it uses. Its calling cards are made of recycled plastic.

The company's 250,000 consumer customers and 3,000

business customers donate to causes such as The Center
for Third World Organizing, Greenpeace, Planned Parenthood, and Artists for a Hate Free America. They receive volume discounts of up to 30 percent in return. They
also receive a 25 percent discount when they call other
Working Assets customers.

The company has created a powerful brand and a lasting bond with its customers. It's a winning strategy. The
company has frequently appeared on *Inc.* magazine's list of
America's 500 fastest-growing private companies.

"We are a values-driven company, but we also really run
it to be an excellent business," Scher says. "If we weren't a
lean organization, we couldn't have weathered things like
our bank telling us they didn't want us to issue any more
credit cards."

The company had a credit-card resale agreement with
State Street Bank in the 1980s, Scher says. The bank thought
Working Assets would sell 10,000 cards during a three-year
period, but it issued that many between March and June of
1986. The bank ended the agreement. Scher said the company, which had just eight employees at the time, couldn't
have survived without its low-cost structure.

George Benson and Airadigm
Building a local PCS brand

George Benson has come a long way since he opened his first business—The Yakima Boys Fruit Stand—on a roadside near Seattle. The 23-year-old entrepreneur was working and going to college on the Korean GI Bill. "We went broke," said Benson, who with his partner sold plenty of apples, but allowed their ambitions to get the best of them. They tried to grow too quickly, and they went bankrupt. They managed to repay all their debts six years later, but they were finished in the fruit business.

Forty years have passed, and Benson is back in business for himself. But this time, he is running a digital wireless phone company in Little Chute, Wisconsin. At 63, he's overcome the urge to grow too quickly. "We're not out there competing with the (mass-market) cellular carriers," Benson says. "We're looking at niche markets." Their focus is mobile wireless phone service for small and medium-size businesses in parts of Wisconsin and Iowa. As CEO of Airadigm,

Benson must maneuver among powerful nationwide carriers such as AT&T Wireless, Sprint Spectrum, and PCS PrimeCo. The industry favors him in one respect. The marketing of wireless service is a local proposition. Competitors, prices, and the needs of customers vary from town to town.

Investments are enormous, though, and smaller companies generally don't have the access to capital that larger companies enjoy. They certainly don't have the same economies of scale. The wireless market has already gotten the best of many smaller carriers. Pocket Communications, a digital wireless company based in Washington, sought protection in bankruptcy court in 1997, and other entrepreneurs have run into difficulty paying for the licenses they bought from the FCC. The share prices of wireless companies took a dive, making it impossible for newcomers to issue stock. The wireless business hasn't been easy for entrepreneurs in recent years.

Airadigm, however, has managed to stay solvent and establish a brand. Benson says the company will become cash-flow positive in 1999. The privately held concern, owned by Wisconsin Wireless Communications Corp., has a steady source of capital. Many wireless carriers have placed their financial well-being in the hands of the fickle capital markets, only to be spurned. Airadigm has raised money from the Oneida tribe of Native Americans. Airadigm spent $60 million to buy 15 PCS licenses, and it is spending $100 million to construct the first phase of its network.

The big PCS carriers have targeted medium and large markets. Airadigm delivers Personal Communications Services to parts of Wisconsin and Iowa, areas that others have largely ignored. Unlike most wireless carriers, who focus on the residential market, Airadigm is targeting small and medium-size businesses. Like many successful entrepreneurs in telecommunications, the company built its niche around the prior experience that management brought to the company. Airadigm does a lot of business, for example, with paper mills in remote towns of the northern Midwest. Benson's relationships with some of these companies date back to one of his earlier enterprises that distributed PBX switching equipment for businesses. After the fruit stand failed, Benson took a sales job with a telecommunications equipment company that was later acquired by NCR. He started his own distribution business in the 1970s, and he switched to telecommunications services around 1986 after reading a news story about the PCS auctions while on an airplane. He has brought that telecommunications experience, and a set of long-standing customers, to Airadigm.

Benson is also maintaining a technological edge. He's positioning his wireless phones as a replacement for traditional wired telephone services. Eventually, Benson argues, businesses will drop the Centrex services they buy from local carriers and use wireless instead. Centrex allows small businesses to duplicate call routing and other advanced features of expensive office systems. Benson says his digital wireless phones, which use the GSM standard, offer the same level of service. Benson likes the GSM phones because they accept computer memory cards that will allow users to load special programs, such as extended phone number directories, directly into their phones.

Airadigm is also launching a new wireless brand. The company markets its service under the Einstein brand, which features a cartoon character that looks like a wireless phone with arms and legs and a big smile. The name conjures up images of intelligence and technological sophistication, tempered with the levity.

Airadigm plans to extend that brand to other services, competing with larger integrated carriers. It has local resale agreements with Ameritech and a number of independent local companies. Resale agreements with long-distance carriers MCI and Frontier have been struck as well. Airadigm is providing Internet access service, too.

Benson is even cautiously thinking about expansion. Some smaller PCS companies that ran into financial trouble may return their licenses to the FCC, which will resell them. "We may rebid for the licenses, depending on what comes available," Benson says. Hopefully, the lessons of the fruit-stand debacle will hold. It could take a lot more than six years to repay the debts of a bankrupt PCS company.

Clark T. Madigan and TeleCom Towers

Location, location, location

Clark Madigan didn't expect much from the broadcasting tower when he and his four partners bought it in 1989. They managed a small investment fund, and they needed a guaranteed source of income to help sustain it. The 540-foot tower on Mermaid Lane in Philadelphia fit the bill. Broadcasting companies had been paying rent since 1946 to install their antennas on the structure, which sits on a prime spot overlooking the city. The group paid $2.6 million for the tower, which had operating margins of more than 70 percent.

The tower was destined to play more than a supporting role in an investment banking concern. "The income from the tower was growing and we didn't know why," said Madigan, 58, a veteran of the telecommunications and banking businesses. It became the star of the operation within months. The group spun off the tower as TeleCom Towers Inc. in 1990. Madigan, a veteran of Marine Midland and the old Manufacturers Hanover bank, quit the investment fund a year later and devoted himself to the new business. He worked the first two-and-a-half years without pay, adding properties to the company's portfolio. "About the time I was running out of money we crossed the line and started making a positive cash flow," says Madigan, president.

TeleCom Towers, based in Arlington, Virginia, is one of hundreds of companies that have filled one of the hottest niches of the telecommunications business: building, leasing, and managing towers and rooftops for the antennas that make the wireless and broadcast industries work. Its growth was fueled by the growth of the wireless business itself. The FCC licensed two cellular carriers in each market in the mid-1980s. The industry grew 50 percent a year, and then things really started to take off. The FCC auctioned additional licenses for Personal Communications Services (PCS), a new mobile digital phone service, in the mid-1990s. That raised the number of competitors in each market to five or six or more. Pagers and specialized mobile radio dispatchers fed the need for antennas, too. Demand for rooftop and tower rights continues to grow with the arrival of "fixed" wireless systems, non-mobile telephones that are wired to building-top antennas. New digital television stations will require yet more antennas.

"We decided the way we want to ride this wave… is to acquire, grow, and build the infrastructure that's needed to run this industry," Madigan says. Now, TeleCom Towers, is one of hundreds of companies across the country that broker real estate for wireless antennas. The company owns 350 towers and manages an additional 500 rooftop and tower sites. It employs 25 people and planned to add 16 by the end of 1997. It also has an engineering subsidiary with a staff of 110.

Environmental Concerns

The business is much more complicated than just building and leasing. "There are environmental issues, concerns over radiation, aesthetic concerns… All of these play into tremendous zoning battles," Madigan says. "Our company helps people find locations and build towers… It's a tough job. Nobody wants a big, ugly tower in their backyard."

The number of communications towers in the country is growing quickly. A few years ago, Madigan estimates, there were 60,000 to 70,000 towers over 200 feet tall and 300,000 towers under that height. There are probably 100,000 taller towers on the landscape today, and a countless number of smaller ones. The number hasn't peaked yet either, and businesses are still entering the infrastructure business. Madigan says the opportunities are still open in the United States, and that they are even bigger in other countries.

There are other ways to play the infrastructure market. Companies specialize in building the steel towers or the prefabricated or concrete utility sheds at their base. Others build antennas or the red airplane warning lights perched on the top.

But the returns in the tower business are hard to beat. Operating margins for rental sites are generally in the 40 percent to 50 percent range. Lease arrangements vary across the country: East Coast landlords often forgo rent in exchange for 60 percent to 80 percent of revenues. Landlords in the West often demand a fixed rental payment of $1,000 to $3,000 a month, although some prefer a combination of rent and revenue. Madigan recommends a long-term lease— five to ten years or longer.

It's more profitable still to own the towers. TeleCom Tower's properties produce average margins of 72 percent. Investments can be substantial, though. A 2,000-foot antenna designed for broadcasting antennas can cost $2.5 million to $3 million. A 300- to 400-foot tower costs about $100,000. The company will also build towers for its clients and lease them back to them, an increasingly popular option. Carriers once preferred to own every aspect of their business. Now they often focus on the core businesses and hire other people to do the rest.

TeleCom Towers charges clients a monthly fee to keep an antenna on one of its sites. A tower can tolerate only so much wind load. Clients pay dearly—as much as $20,000 a month—to install TV antennas and other large pieces of equipment that put a lot of stress on the tower. Cellular and PCS companies pay about $600 to $2,500 a month; paging companies, $300 to $1,200; private radio systems, $300 to $500.

A PCS Generated Need

PCS really drove the need for more antennas. These small digital wireless phones use less power than older cellular phones, allowing people to talk longer before their battery runs out of power. The trade-off is that they can't transmit over long distances, and PCS operators must build more antennas to boost phone signals. The original cellular system in Washington required about 30 antennas. New PCS systems in the same region require 650 smaller antennas, many of them 150- to 200-foot structures that fit on a rooftop, TeleCom Towers says.

Wireless carriers can easily spend billions of dollars on infrastructure. A PCS carrier planning a modest 200-site system can pay TeleCom Towers $150,000 a site to find locations, negotiate the purchase or the land lease, and construct the sites. That's $30 million. "The infrastructure costs are enormous," Madigan says. "On top of that, the PCS carrier paid dearly for its license." That doesn't include marketing costs either. Considering all those costs, Madigan is glad to be on the infrastructure side of the business.

TeleCom Towers is growing quickly, too, at 45 percent a year. Revenues hit $15 million in 1997, and the company had $10 million to $11 million in operating cash flow. It plans to go public as revenues reach the $20 million to $25 million range, market conditions permitting. It raised $50 million by selling a 49 percent stake to Cox Enterprises in October 1997. "I think what we are seeing today is just scratching the surface," Madigan says. "These technological changes must play out around the world. The international side is going to be enormous."

But he may never find another tower as valuable as the World War II-era tower in Philadelphia. The company turned down $5.5 million for it in 1997. It's generating cash flow of $750,000 a year, and Madigan figures it's worth $7.5 million to $8 million. "I don't think we ever expected operating margins like this," he says.

Pasha Roberts and Webline Communications

Telemarketing on the Web

First came the door-to-door salesman. Then came the phone-to-phone salesman, or the telemarketer. The next stage in the evolution of one-on-one sales will be computer-to-computer: salesman and consumer conversing over the Web.

Pasha Roberts and Firdaus Bhathena developed the business plan for Webline Communications while they were graduate students at MIT in 1995. Their goal was to extend the commercial capabilities of the Web, which functioned as little more than a series of billboards plastered on Web pages instead of on roadside scaffolds. The idea was to breathe life into the Web by allowing company and customer to communicate as if they were on the telephone. They developed Java programs that would allow a salesman to take control of a customer's computer screen, delivering information via a Web browser. The customer doesn't need any special hardware or software to use the service. Customer and salesman can hold a simultaneous conversation over the phone. There's a potential for video communication in the future, as computers and phone networks are upgraded.

"We have added a visual component to telemarketing," says Roberts, 35. "I can actually take control of your browser and add anything I want to the screen, record whatever is going on and complete a sale."

The technology could also be used for teleconferencing or customer service, although Webline is limiting itself to telemarketing. "There are a lot of applications for this technology. The important thing for us is to keep focused," Roberts says. "As a company with six people, you can't go in 20 directions."

Roberts and Bhathena plan to market Webline to financial companies, and possibly to travel companies and call-centers. "The selling proposition has to be very specific," Roberts says. "It isn't useful for selling knives. It *is* useful for buying a mutual fund."

Roberts, a business school student, and Bhathena, won MIT's annual business plan contest. They won $50,000 worth of cash and in-kind services, plus invaluable attention that led to $1 million worth of seed money from venture capitalists. As of early 1997, the company was operating out of a 1,700-square-foot office with more computers than people. Roberts described it as "not quite a dump." Everyone was working on reduced salaries in exchange for equity in the company. Experienced engineers command at least $80,000 or $90,000 a year, but most people were working for one-third to one-half that amount. The bulk of the budget was going toward salary and headhunter fees. The company signed up its first major customer in early 1997, a high-tech textbook and software maker named Course Technology.

Gaining 'Investor Credibility'

The company raised an additional $3 million in venture capital as the year rolled on. It also hired an experienced CEO, Avid Technology veteran Dan Keshian. Roberts, who started the year as president, finished it as architect, computer telephony integration. Roberts knew all along that he wouldn't be running Webline. "It's necessary for the kind of company we want to build, there's just no other way to… get investor credibility," he says. "If it were going to be a $20 million company, I could probably do that. To bring it to the multi-hundred-million level, we need to bring in an experienced CEO."

Keshian built Avid from zero to $400 million a year in revenue in a few years, and Webline has similar ambitions. Roberts expects the company to be profitable after the first year or two. He projects that revenues will hit the multi-hundred-million level in four or five years. It's positioned for an IPO. An acquisition is a possibility, but Roberts says that isn't the main goal.

Roberts witnessed the birth of the Internet as a child in Washington. His father, Larry Roberts—head of the Defense Department's Advanced Research Projects department—was one of the key architects of the Internet, and hired BBN Corp. to build ARPANET, the precursor to the Internet. "At parties, anyway, I can say I was on the Internet in 1969. What I remember is playing games on it. It was before e-mail and before the Web. It was like news groups."

Roberts spent 11 years as a software developer, including a stint at Boston's Brigham and Women's Hospital. Then he went to MIT. "We think this concept is going to be around a while," Roberts says. "Some people talk about how Internet telephony is going to eliminate the phone. I think the jury is still out. We think there is a lot of opportunity in the short to medium range to get some telemarketing opportunities out."

Bob Gold and Transaction Information Systems

Paving the way for electronic commerce

Electronic commerce is in its infancy. Bob Gold of Transaction Information Systems (TIS) is nurturing its growth, and he expects to raise a monster. A mere $2 billion in goods and services exchanged hands in cyberspace in 1997, according to Gold's estimates. Gold expects electronic commerce to hit $200 to $300 billion in the next five to seven years, transforming the economy and beyond.

"As the infrastructure of the U.S. gets upgraded in the next year to five years, all these things will be more practical and will change the way people work and live," says the 39-year-old software writer and entrepreneur. "The infrastructure is coming. The question is, how will people take advantage of that?"

He has carved out a huge market for himself by creating

the economic infrastructure of the future. Working from a landmark building in lower Manhattan, TIS writes programs that are bringing the financial industry into the age of the Internet. Applications include securities trading to banking, 401(k) retirement plans, and customer service. Clients such as Prudential Insurance buy a single program that can be run over a range of devices: PCs, televisions, telephones, and information kiosks. The whirring computers in the vault-like offices, built in 1909 by the New York Lawyers Club, provide a counterpoint to a massive stained-glass window and gargoyles and mahogany arches. The site is also home to Gold's latest project, the Financial Lab for Interactive Technology (FLITE). Its 23 "member" companies—which include IBM, Visa, Bell Atlantic Mobile, and Sybase—conduct experiments and showcase their technology at the open-standards computer laboratory. They developed the latest in Web-based customer service systems and three-dimensional charts for displaying financial data.

Operating largely beyond the view of the business press and the investment world, the privately held company has blossomed during the last five years. Revenues were expected to reach $55 millon in 1997, up from just $2 millon in the first year. "And I don't think we've even gotten started yet," Gold says. It ranks 103 on *Inc.* magazine's list of the fastest growing private companies in the United States. The company, with just two employees at the beginning, now employs 500. Remarkably, the company is entirely self-financed. Gold and co-founder Jeff Najarian began with a string of consulting assignments and poured the money back into the business. They didn't tap the venture-capital world, let alone the capital markets.

Gold left Rutgers University with a master's degree in computer science and ambitions in the corporate world. His career path led him through Digital Equipment, Northern Telecom, and Nynex. He was on track for a hot career with a big corporation, but he left it behind to become an entrepreneur. His specialty was transactional applications, software programs that allow people to do business over computer networks. He created complex programs that managed enormous amounts of data and required high levels of security. Only a few big companies could afford to run them on their networks, because they cost $50,000 or $100,000 per computer. So Gold had a vision: bring this technology to the mass market. "What I saw was a technology that had great appeal to the masses, and there was not a good distribution vehicle for those smaller- to medium-size businesses and consumers to take advantage of," he says.

TIS's early products, created just before the emergence of the Internet, were written according to private standards. But Gold immediately understood the potential of the World Wide Web, an open, public standard that could be used to distribute his technology to the masses.

"We retooled for the Internet, and that is what made the business take off," he says. The company's rapid growth shows how the Internet has created new businesses and industries in the blink of an eye.

He sees four broad areas of opportunity:

- Creating the technology that makes electronic commerce possible, as TIS is doing now.

- Creating "content" that rides the network.

- Selling devices that the public uses to access the network.

- Building or operating telecommunications infrastructure.

The best entrepreneurs get their start by pursuing a passion in one of these areas, establishing a foundation for future expansion. "You always have to do one thing well and be passionate about it," he says. "Passion makes the best entrepreneurs. Those people are really successful."

The first step is to find a niche and master it. That establishes a foundation for a more long-term business plan, he says. "You have to leverage (a niche) into other things over time. Otherwise, growth becomes tougher and tougher."

Microsoft has evolved according to this pattern. The giant software company, having mastered the world of operating systems and software applications, is expanding into the realm known as "content." Bill Gates has invested in a cable television network and Web site, MSNBC, and an on-line magazine called *Slate*. He has also invested $1 billion in Comcast, which operates cable TV systems.

Gold plans a similar expansion for TIS. The company has been exploring the creation of content for the financial and entertainment industries. He sees big opportunity there. Programmers won't need to be as big as Disney in the near future. There will be thousands of smaller programming companies operating in spaces that aren't used for programming today. A few years from now, for example, a home builder might prepare a weekly show broadcast exclusively at a kiosk in the aisle of a local building supply store. The show would have promotional value for the builder and the retailer. Live demonstrations and videotaped demonstrations are already common.

People don't need to be computer specialists to thrive in this environment. There will also be a tremendous need for people with media skills. "Understanding a particular kind of content isn't as important as understanding what it takes to build and deploy content. That is what you need to understand," Gold says. "You need to combine an understanding of the technology with an understanding of how to make a movie or a TV show. What was the workflow and the dynamic that made it profitable? If I can develop content first, I can find distribution channels for it. That is the crux of it."

Gold clearly envisions an enterprise of enormous scope, growing quickly alongside the digital economy. "It took five years to build the infrastructure," Gold says. "Now we're going to blow it out."

Marc Andreessen and Netscape Communications

Viewing telecommunications from Silicon Valley

The telecommunications industry was blindsided by the Internet, which seemed to appear from nowhere in 1994. Now the cofounder of the company that led the revolution warns the telecommunications industry that it is at risk once again from software companies poaching on its turf.

"The interesting thing to me is that it was so easy," muses Marc Andreessen, the 26-year-old cofounder of Netscape Communications. He led the development of the Mosaic Web browser that was incorporated into Netscape software. "It's amazing to me that one of these big companies didn't do it," he said. "It was just a couple kids in a research lab. There wasn't anything tough about it. The big companies just weren't paying attention. They were pursuing grander things, like interactive television, and most of them are still catching up."

Marc Andreessen

Andreessen surveyed the Internet in 1991 and decided there had to be a better way. Just a few years earlier, the typical computer screen had been a murky, black abyss with ugly, green type, and software programs were controlled with long and arcane strings of letters and symbols. The Macintosh and Windows operating systems changed all that: The screen became a desktop; the digital document was redesigned to look like a piece of paper. The pieces of paper were organized into folders, just like in the real world, or someone's image of it. The awkward typewritten commands were replaced with pictures. If you wanted to delete a file, you clicked your mouse on the picture of the file and dragged it to the picture of a trash can. This new way of doing things, known as a graphical user interface (GUI), made computers easier to use. The Internet, the network that linked millions of computers around the world, was stuck in the past.

Andreessen, a student at the University of Illinois at Champagne-Urbana, yearned for a better Internet. He wasn't the only person who envisioned something better. "I worked at a research lab with high-energy physics experts. The Internet was pervasive. It was how they contacted their colleagues around the world," Andreessen recalls. "The PC had become easy to use, but the Internet was still very cryptic and hard to use. It became clear that someone needed to take the graphical user interface and wed it to the Internet."

So he did.

Andreessen, who worked at the National Center for Supercomputing Applications (NCSA), tackled the job in his spare time with a few colleagues. "We just decided to go ahead with it," he says. "It wasn't even clear there was a commercial opportunity. That came much later."

The group built on ideas that had already been proposed. "Most new things are a synthesis of things already out there," he says. Big companies sometimes miss the importance of these things because they don't have immediate and obvious commercial potential, according to Andreessen.

An experimental copy of NCSA Mosaic was finished in three months. The group posted a message on the Internet, asking if anyone wanted to try it. About a dozen people responded by e-mail requesting copies. They distributed copies to their friends, and their friends passed them along to others. Other browsers were available—text mode browsers and browsers with alternative interfaces—but Mosaic eliminated the need to know lots of arcane acronyms and command-line options.

"It was just a case of word of mouth. The Net itself was propagation," Andreessen says. Meanwhile, hundreds of Internet users sent e-mail messages with suggestions for improving the program. It quickly caught the attention of the business world, too. Andreessen started to receive inquiries from such companies as Sun Microsystems, which wanted to license the program and distribute it with its products.

Andreessen graduated from Illinois in 1993 with a Bachelor of Science degree and headed off to Silicon Valley. He landed a job at a company called Enterprise Integration Technologies, which conducted research funded by the Defense Department's Advanced Research Projects Agency, the government group that created the Internet in the late 1960s. The company has been merged into Hewlett Packard in recent years.

"If I'd stayed there, I would be one of thousands of HP people," Andreessen muses. But he got a call within three months from Jim Clark instead. Clark was ready to leave Silicon Graphics, the company he founded 12 years earlier. He wanted to start a software company, and to staff it with people from outside Silicon Graphics, lest he disrupt the business. He wanted to know if Andreessen would be interested in starting a new company that would develop Internet-based consumer and commercial applications.

Clark provided the first round of financing. Then they turned to the influential venture-capital firm of Kleiner Perkins Caufield & Byers, which had also launched Sun. Clark and Andreessen raised an additional round of funding from cable company TCI and Adobe software, but they never needed it.

Netscape recruited a seasoned CEO, Jim Barkesdale of McCaw Cellular Communications. He had also spent a dozen years as chief information officer at Federal Express, which had developed powerful package-tracking systems on its computer network. "If you are going to build a serious business, the management team is the critical part. It's important that the founders take the right role and not try to be things they are not," Andreessen says.

A Spectacular IPO

Netscape Communications proceeded directly to one of the most spectacular initial public offerings in history. Netscape distributed 2 million copies of its browser during its first year of operation. The effect was overwhelming. Within months, pioneering companies were erecting corporate Web sites, and including their Web addresses on billboards for all the public to see. The on-line services—such as America Online, CompuServe, and Prodigy—scrapped their closed networks. They shifted their technology to the Web, basically becoming Internet-access providers that helped members sift through the chaos of the Web.

AT&T, which had bought a private on-line service from *The Washington Post* just a year before, scrapped its plans, took a $50 million write-off, and started its own Internet-access service, WorldNet. And Microsoft, sensing that Netscape was a serious threat to its dominance of the desktop, created a Web browser of its own, Explorer, in short. The Internet started to grow at an astonishing 1000 percent a year. Netscape's stock began trading in 1994. It rose like a rocket, and Andreessen's stake is now worth about $42 million.

Even as telecommunications companies grapple with the emergence of the Web, a new threat looms. The long-term migration from analog circuit-switched networks to packet-based networks will reorder the telecommunications industry along radically different lines, Andreessen says. Only this time, the interloper isn't a small start-up venture. It's Microsoft.

"Microsoft tries to commoditize everything below it," Andreessen says of his giant rival in Seattle. "If Microsoft succeeds, the telecom companies will provide bandwidth and Microsoft will provide higher services." Of course, Andreessen understands Microsoft's market power as well as anyone. Microsoft arrived a little late to the Internet, but not too late to catch up with Netscape's once ubiquitous browser. Telecom companies run the risk that Microsoft will move the guts of the telecommunications industry from the network to the desktop, replacing a lot of the functions of the network switch.

Andreessen envisions the telecommunications industry segmenting into horizontal levels such as those of the PC industry, where some companies specialize in PC hardware, others specialize in networking, and others specialize in software programs and applications. The big question is, will the companies that provide the pipes of the telecommunications network be stuck with a commodity, and will those companies also provide specialized applications that ride the network? "Microsoft could suck lots of value out of the telecom companies because it (the network) will be reconstructed as software," Andreessen says.

Microsoft, Cisco, Dialogix, U.S. Robotics, and VocalTec met in 1996 to establish a voice in Internet Protocol (IP) that establishes a standard for direct computer-server to computer-server voice communications, Price Waterhouse notes in its 1998 Technology Forecast. "Internet players are now making forays into traditional PSTN (Public Switched Telephone Network) applications," Price Waterhouse says. "Today, Internet telephony and videoconferencing are still experimental, but they are gaining user acceptance as quality increases."

Internet faxing, which draws traffic off the phone network, is just the beginning. Vienna Systems, for example, is offering a new system that combines voice, data, and video on a corporate local-area network. "The server software establishes and manages all calls and provides telephony features such as call hold and call forwarding," Price Waterhouse says. Those sorts of enhanced features are controlled by phone companies today, and account for much of their projected future profits. Revenues from enhanced features are growing about 30 percent a year, and phone companies can't afford to lose them.

Andreessen says phone companies and telecom entrepreneurs should start acting and thinking more like companies in Silicon Valley. "My biggest advice watching all these companies… (is to) focus on something immediate and practical. Get to market as fast as possible. Don't try to build the perfect product. Get to market and build mind share and momentum."

Bernie Ebbers and WorldCom

*From small-town entrepreneur
to corporate kingpin*

Bernie Ebbers is not given to expounding on theory. He doesn't offer grand explanations for WorldCom's success or advice for others. "I can only talk about *my* experience," he says. But what an experience it has been!

He has gone from gym teacher to CEO of a $6 billion company that is in the process of closing the largest corporate deal in history, the acquisition of MCI. WorldCom has the second best performance record, after Oracle, on Wall Street. A $100 investment in the company in 1989 was worth $2,200 at the end of 1996. Ebbers conducted 50 acquisitions in the last five years, assembling a futuristic collection of assets including UUNet Technologies, the world's largest Internet services company, and MFS, which provides local service to businesses over its own fiber networks. Ebbers also created the fourth largest long-distance carrier in the United States, and that doesn't include MCI. With a

Bernie Ebbers

strong orientation toward packet-switching, data services, and the Internet, the company has pushed into Europe and Asia, too.

With a quiet, hard demeanor and a saber-like wit, Ebbers has also shaken the staid, clubby atmosphere of the $670 billion global telecommunications business. As he launched his MCI campaign from a hotel room in Manhattan, Ebbers announced that MCI chairman Bert Roberts was welcome to join the new company, but that he would have to show up for work a little earlier. He told rival suitor British Telecommunications that it was welcome to join forces in a three-way deal, "if they can behave themselves."

Ebbers' experience traces an unlikely course across North America. He was born and raised in Ottawa, and he ventured south to Mississippi on a basketball scholarship. He graduated with plans to teach high school science and gym. The pay was low, and Ebbers eventually took a job managing a garment warehouse. "I didn't have much vision for my own personal future for quite some time," he says. "I had an opportunity to work in the garment business for a few years. I decided I would try that and see if I could make a living. I never had any idea this would ever happen."

The warehouse allowed him to make some money for the first time, and that stoked the smoldering embers of ambition nurtured by the three men who influenced him most: his father; his high school, coach John Baker; and his college coach, James Allen. "My high school coach taught me there was more to life than doing nothing," Ebbers says. "And my college coach taught me that, with hard work, dedication, a commitment to principles, and a commitment to Jesus Christ, life can be worthwhile."

He entered the motel business six years later. The turning point came in 1983, just before the breakup of AT&T. A friend approached him with a plan for a long-distance telephone business. Ebbers was impressed with the cash-flow potential, and he made a passive investment, hoping to raise funds so he could buy more motels. "It was not intended to be a large investment," he says. "At that point in time, I didn't care about the business at all."

The company, known as LDDS, was a failure at first. Desperate and teetering on the brink of bankruptcy, the board asked Ebbers to become CEO. The mission was minimal: Sell the company. No one was interested in buying it, though; they were stuck with the company and had to close it down or make it grow. "We decided, if we were going to repay the bank loan, we were going to have to try to make it work," he says. "After I got involved in it, I started seeing some of the potential."

The focus of the company has always been the creation of shareholder value. "My ambitions for WorldCom are to continue to be the premier performance stock on Wall Street," he says. That ambition created a financial logic that shaped the company. That sort of shareholder wealth requires a company of great scale and scope. The economics of the business required him to invest in networks and grow globally. "It required us to be a fast-growing international company."

International Barriers Removed

Ebbers believes that the opportunities are far bigger now than they were in 1983, thanks to changes in technology and regulation. "The opportunities were in long-distance because of regulatory issues, divestiture (of AT&T), and so on," he says. "Now the opportunities are in a much more expanded area. The international barriers are coming down. It's becoming a worldwide business. Local competition is coming, albeit rather slowly, which gives us more opportunity than we had in long-distance."

He sees huge potential opportunities in the consumer market, too, if the regulatory issues can be resolved. "Yes, there is going to be a great opportunity in the consumer market in the future," Ebbers says. "The question is, how do you get to serve those customers? Those issues are being worked out at this moment in time."

WorldCom's decision to buy MCI for $34 billion was driven partly by MCI's number two position in the U.S. consumer long-distance business. The companies were awaiting regulatory approval as 1997 ended.

Ebbers sees opportunity selling consumers local, long-distance, and video services. The economics of the consumer sector are a challenge, though. "You can't build your own network in a large part of the residential marketplace because the density of traffic does not justify the investment. That's the problem," Ebbers says, adding that the only mass-market alternative is to resell the service of the dominant local carriers. The wholesale prices are economically viable, Ebbers says, blaming the Eighth Circuit Court of Appeals for overturning the FCC's pricing guidelines.

There is some evidence of competition in the local sector despite the economic difficulties. "It's starting already; RCN is doing quite an excellent job in that," Ebbers says. He even held out the possibility of a partnership with the company, building on ties that go back several years. RCN CEO David McCourt was associated with MFS Communications, which was acquired by WorldCom in 1996, and McCourt has held a position on WorldCom's board. Ebbers says he isn't likely to start building his own networks in the consumer market. "We will probably work with people like that," he says.

Ebbers also is working hard to keep MCI executives in the new company. Their knowledge of the consumer market is irreplaceable. WorldCom has had a mixed record of holding onto key executives from other acquisitions. MCI is spending about $500,000 on bonuses for managers it wants to keep, and Ebbers gave MCI's Roberts the title of chairman. When MCI and WorldCom finally announced an agreement that ended the bidding war with BT and GTE, Ebbers stood on a dias and referred to Roberts as "bossman."

"One of the real problems a lot of entrepreneurs have is that they think they know a lot more than they really do," Ebbers says. "It is important to have an honest evaluation of one's own capabilities, and make sure that (in areas) where you are not fully capable you bring in people who are. I guess, don't overestimate what you think you know."

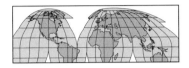

Appendices

The Telecommunications Act

The seeds of the Telecommunications Act were planted in 1984 when the regional Bell phone companies were spun off from AT&T. The breakup preserved the decades-old idea that local phone service was a *natural monopoly*, which is economic jargon for something that is too expensive to duplicate. Most of the nation's local phone business was turned over to seven regional holding companies—Nynex, Bell Atlantic, BellSouth, Ameritech, US West, Southwestern Bell, and Pacific Telesis—which controlled nearly all the local phone service in their territories. The government tried to prevent these powerful companies from abusing their monopolies by restricting them from other lines of business, such as long-distance and equipment manufacturing.

The Bells wanted to escape these restrictions from the very start and, by the mid-1990s, the debate began to swing in their direction. These big companies' inherent political power stemmed from their widely dispersed customers, operations, and work forces. The prevailing political ideas of the day were shifting in their favor, too. Governments everywhere were increasingly receptive to the idea that competitive markets were better regulators than government bureaucrats. The rallying call of the free market was sounded from the Reagan-Bush White House to Eastern Europe, Russia, and China. The old monopoly structure of the telecommunications industry was out of step with the times. Technology strengthened that conviction: It appeared that electric utilities, cable TV companies, satellite services, and other new media were ready to compete with the local phone companies, and that the competitive market would lead to lower prices and better services.

In August 1994, the Senate Commerce Committee approved a bill that would have allowed the Bells into long-distance, but it died because it imposed tough conditions on their freedom. The balance of power shifted in the Bells' favor a few months later when Republicans took control of both the Senate and the House of Representatives for the first time in 40 years. Work on a new telecommunications bill began in early 1995. The legislation gave way to the Bells on almost every major point. It didn't allow them to enter the long-distance phone market until they proved to state regulators and the FCC that their local markets were open to competition. However, the test wasn't too tough, the main condition being that the Bells must face a competitor doing business largely over an independent network. The presence of a mere reseller isn't enough. But the law doesn't require the Bells to lose a specific amount of market share before they enter long-distance. That was a major victory for the Bells and a major loss for the long-distance carriers.

The Bells also won a crucial battle over the role of the Justice Department, which was limited to a consultative role in deciding when the Bells have passed the test. The long-distance carriers wanted a greater role for the Justice Department, which is responsible for enforcing antitrust rules and is naturally inclined to take a strict view of Bell expansion into long-distance. The Justice Department was limited to a consultative role. The rules clearly favor the Bells and GTE, but the implementation of the rules has been slower than the Bells predicted. The FCC hadn't allowed any of the Bells into the long-distance market as of late 1997, and several Bells have sued the agency over its strict interpretation of the rules. The courts have ruled in the Bells favor so far, but the decisions are still under appeal.

Entering the Local Market

The big beneficiaries of the law itself included the Bells and GTE and entrepreneurs in the local market. The interests of the big, established local companies and the newcomers were thrown together. The big players need small companies to help them establish that their markets are competitive, allowing them to qualify for the long-distance market. The law created three ways for companies to enter the local market.

Total service resale: This allows a competitor to buy local service lock, stock, and barrel from a dominant carrier at a discount set by state regulators, usually about 20 percent. It includes access to switches, transmission lines, and all other network elements. The competitor resells the service to customers under its own name. AT&T, MCI, and other large newcomers to the local market wanted discounts of 35 to 40 percent, asserting that the current economics of total service resale didn't allow them to make a profit. Nonetheless, some entrants use it to establish a quick market presence. Other companies believe the economics will improve as competition increases.

Unbundled network elements: Competitors can also lease bits and pieces of another carrier's network, filling in the gaps in their own partially constructed facilities. It's similar to a homeowner who keeps a basic set of tools around the house for routine jobs, and leases more specialized tools from an equipment rental store as the need arises. A telecommunications company might install its own switches, but lease transmission lines from the local Bell company. Or it might install its own transmission lines in lucrative financial districts and lease lines in less lucrative residential neighborhoods. The margins are often around 40 percent, roughly twice as high as total service resale.

Network construction: By maintaining total resale margins at a low level, and by requiring the Bells to allow competition from newcomers with their own switches and transmission lines, the government has encouraged the construction of new facilities. Capital costs require access to substantial amounts of capital, but the investments generate operating margins of 60 percent. The law also allows network-based entrepreneurs to resell their networks to other carriers and charge higher rates than the Bells can charge. The Bells, GTE, and other independent phone companies base their resale rates on the retail price of local phone service, minus the cost of marketing, billing, collection, and other costs that are picked up by the competing carrier. Entrepreneurs who build new local networks are allowed to base their resale rates on a different, somewhat more favorable, formula that allows them to recoup costs and make a profit.

Terms of Business

The law establishes tight limits on the Bells, but entrepreneurs are free to enter any sector of telecommunications they wish, from long-distance and local service to cable television, equipment manufacturing, and Internet access. They don't have to prove they are qualified to compete in certain areas, which the Bells must do. Once they enter the market, they must abide by a number of conditions established by the Telecommunications Act. Just as the Bells, GTE, and other incumbent phone companies must negotiate their coexistence with newcomers, those very newcomers must negotiate agreements of coexistence with other phone companies. They must come to terms on a host of issues within 135 days after the interconnection request is made. Otherwise, the newcomer can ask state regulators to arbitrate.

The topics of negotiation include:

Interconnection: The Telecom Act says that all telecommunications companies must agree to connect their networks with all other telecom companies. That's significant and new. A local phone company can't force its customers to buy long-distance service from a particular affiliate. It must connect its network to all local and long-distance carriers. The physical connection must be made at any technically feasible point that the competitor prefers. Companies must allow their competitors access to their offices and field sites so that the physical connection can be made.

Resale: All carriers must make their networks available to competitors for total service resale or sale of unbundled network elements. There are several exceptions to the rules on unbundled network elements. Entrepreneurs should be aware of them, since they limit access to existing local networks in significant parts of the country. Carriers aren't required to make proprietary network elements available for resale. And services that were designed specifically for the consumer or business markets can only be resold in those markets. Rural phone companies are exempt from the obligation to unbundle their networks. Rural carriers serve areas that don't have any towns with more than 10,000 people in them, or have less than 50,000 phone lines. Local phone companies that serve less than 2 percent of the country's phone lines can also ask the FCC for an exemption to the unbundling rules.

Dialing parity: The Telecom Act also forbids carriers from forcing competitors' customers to dial extra digits when they make a local call, as AT&T used to do in the long-distance market. People of a certain age will remember the automatic-dialing machines that MCI distributed to its customers in an effort to overcome the inconvenience of the special codes. There is one major exception. Dialing parity is delayed in certain local toll markets. Local toll calls, which travel too far to be local but not far enough to qualify as long-distance, have been a cash cow for local phone companies for years. Local carriers aren't required to institute dialing parity in their local toll markets until 1999 or until they enter the long-distance market, whichever is sooner.

There are, of course, exceptions to the exception, such as creating two groups of states with local toll markets that are more hospitable to entrepreneurs. Fifteen states mandated dialing parity for local toll calls by December 19, 1995, and their orders stand. They include Alaska, Arizona, Connecticut, Florida, Georgia, Illinois, Kentucky, Michigan, Minnesota, New Jersey, New York, Pennsylvania, West Virginia, Wisconsin, and Wyoming. The act also allows an additional group of less populated states, including Delaware, Hawaii, Maine, New Hampshire, New Mexico, Rhode Island, South Dakota, and Vermont, to mandate dialing parity for local toll calls as soon as they please.

Number portability: Carriers must allow their customers to keep their old phone number when they switch to a competing carrier. This obligation doesn't kick in right away, because the industry is still developing the computer programs that will make true number portability work. The industry has been relying on elaborate call forwarding systems that transfer calls to a new number known only by the network. The customer gets to use the old number. The call forwarding technique is an interim solution because it requires a slight delay while the call is transferred.

Reciprocal compensation: In a monopoly market, local calls begin and end on the same network and one company gets all the revenue. In a competitive local market, calls begin on one company's network and end on another, and the carriers must figure out a way to share revenue generated by the call. The Telecom Act may favor the entrepreneur in this instance, too, depending on how the FCC and the courts interpret the law. The question is whether the Bells and the other incumbent local carriers will be allowed to figure the enormous cost of building their network into the payment system, or whether they will simply share in the immediate direct costs of carrying a given call, which are tiny. The question is comparable to this: Do members of a car-pool chip in for gas and tolls, or do they share in the cost of the car itself? The difference is huge. The FCC ruled against the Bells, but the Eighth Circuit Court of Appeals overturned the rules. The federal government and AT&T have since asked the Supreme Court to review the cases. A similar disagreement underlies the debate over resale rates as well.

Rights-of-way: The incumbent local phone companies acquired rights-of-way to construct their networks over the years, and the Telecom Act says they must share them, along with their access to phone poles, ducts, and conduits. They may charge a government-regulated fee to offset their cost. It may seem like a trivial matter, but it's not. The wireless industry operates without any obligation to share rights-of-way, forcing carriers to battle local governments and property owners for the right to erect antennas. The battle over rights-of-way has brought the wireless industry to a standstill in some cases. Competition in the local market wouldn't stand a chance if companies didn't have to share their property rights. Entrepreneurs must share their rights-of-way, too, but they have one advantage over the incumbents: The fees they charge aren't regulated under the Telecom Act, although state regulators can set limits.

Notice of change: Carriers must also notify each other of network changes that effect interconnection. If a local carrier moves a switching facility, for example, it must notify competitors that use the same site.

Other Provisions

The new law imposed numerous other important changes in the phone market, as well. The act:

- ⊡ Allows electric utilities to offer telecommunications service through separate subsidiaries without asking the Securities and Exchange Commission for permission.

- ⊡ Mandates that companies can't charge for information provided during a toll-free call unless they meet several conditions, such as obtaining advance permission or broadcasting a warning during the call.

- ⊡ Limits the use of data that local phone companies gather about their customers to phone service.

- ⊡ Requires long-distance companies to verify that a customer has switched carriers and requires the FCC to establish new regulations to guard against unauthorized changes.

- ⊡ Increases the amount of money that long-distance companies contribute to pay-phone operators, to compensate them for carrying toll-free and emergency service calls. The Telecommunications Act has left several important markets to their own devices. It has little to say about the operation of the Internet. Big phone companies wanted to subject the Internet to taxes and force it to share in the access charges that phone companies pay each other for handing off calls, but they lost their bid. The law did restrict the transmission of smut in cyberspace, but the Supreme Court struck down the restrictions.

The act also required the FCC to establish a new system for funding phone service in rural and low-income customers. Entrepreneurs who enter the market must pay into the system, which was still under development by the FCC in 1997. Entrepreneurs who decide to offer service in rural areas are eligible to receive subsidies.

The law left wireless and data largely to their own devices. Proponents of the free market are quick to point out that these industries are among the fastest growing in the world. The wireless market was shaped by other laws. The price of mobile wireless phone service was deregulated in 1993, giving a boost to the competitive pressures within the market. The FCC auctioned additional wireless phone licenses in the mid-1990s, raising the number of wireless carriers in a given market to eight from two. The Telecommunications Act imposes just a few conditions on wireless mobile service. It requires wireless carriers to connect their networks to all other telecom carriers. And it gives the FCC the power to regulate wireless companies as local exchange carriers, if and when wireless phones become interchangeable with traditional phones. Wireless phone companies must also contribute to the Universal Service Fund, which subsidizes the cost of phone service for rural areas and low-income customers.

The Telecom Act makes substantial changes in the cable TV business. It lifts some of the price controls that were reimposed on the market in 1992, after a brief experiment with deregulation. The law deregulates the price of premium cable services by March 31, 1999. Prices are deregulated earlier in markets where the phone company provides an alternative television service. The law also allows cable companies to enter the phone market, and vice versa. The industries are moving tentatively into each other's markets. In fact, US West decided to spinoff its cable unit in late 1997, reflecting that the once-convergent industries may be diverging after all.

The law also allows local phone companies to enter the video business under a variety of rules. They can operate under the same rules that cable companies follow, controlling all the channels on their system in exchange for following price regulations. They can also share a certain percentage of the channels on their systems with competitors, in exchange for price deregulation. The second option is known as an *open video system*. The law gave a boost to cable's greatest competition, the direct broadcast satellite industry, by forbidding local governments from taxing the service.

The law imposed sweeping and controversial changes in the broadcast industry, too. The law gave television makers two years to install computer chips, known as V-Chips, that can be used to block violent shows. It also drew fire from consumer groups by eliminating limits on the number of radio and television stations a company can own nationally, and it allows greater, but not unlimited, concentration at the local level. That is, there is no limit on the total number of stations a company can operate around the country, but there are limits on the number of stations a company can own in a particular market. The law also authorized the FCC to set aside spectrum for new digital television signals. The law gave a boost to the direct broadcast satellite industry, which competes with cable television. It allows the FCC to regulate the industry, preempting some local ordinances that restricted the use of antennas.

The new law strongly favors the Baby Bells, which will get into long-distance without endangering their local business, analyst Scott Cleland said in a 1996 report for the Washington Research Group. Entrepreneurs in the local market benefit from the Telecommunications Act, too, says Cleland, now head of Legg Mason Wood Walker's Precursor Group. The law focuses on the expansion of the Bells into the local market The law effects the Bells most of all, but it designates a major role for start-up companies. That's because the Bells can't enter the long-distance market until they face local competitors that operate mostly over their own networks. The Bells are depending on smaller companies, known as *competitive access providers*, to establish a record of competition in their local markets. For further information, read the *Telecommunications Act Handbook: A Complete Resource for Business*, edited by Leon T. Krauer, et. al. (Government Institutes, Inc., Rockville, Maryland).

Telecommunications Regulatory Requirements

The following information was provided by Visiology, Inc., 16061 Carmel Bay Drive, Northport, Alabama 35475:

Even though the reseller does not manage, control, operate, own, or lease any telecommunication facilities, most state public utility commissions have chosen to regulate the reseller. Regulation of the resale of telecommunication services varies by commission. We can group that regulation into four categories:

(1) not regulated.
(2) registration required.
(3) certification required.
(4) certification with hearing required.

The information provided in the following pages is based on relevant state commission orders, notices, rules, and similar documents as well as telephone discussions with responsible commission staff members. The requirements shown are for a "typical" switchless reseller reselling 1+ traffic. In today's regulatory environment, the rules and regulations are changing frequently, and the actions of some commissions are subject to differing interpretations. Thus, the information provided herein, while considered to be generally reliable as of the date indicated, is not guaranteed. The chart provides the regulatory requirements for a typical switchless reseller. However, it should not be used to determine the requirements for an actual company. State requirements may vary based on the reseller's services, pricing strategy, and method of operation.

Typical Requirements for 1+ Switchless Resellers by Jurisdiction

State	Certification	Tariff	Cost Support	Attend Hearing	Attorney	Filing Fees	Time Estimate	Certificate of Foreign Corp[1]	Registered Agent[2]
AK [3]	yes	yes	no	no	no	$0	90 Days	no	no
AL	yes	yes	no	yes	recommend [4]	$0	3 Months	yes	yes
AR	yes	yes	no	no	no	$200	2 - 3 Months	yes	yes
AZ [5]	yes	yes	no	no	no	$0	6 - 9 Months	no[6]	no
CA [7]	yes	no[8]	no	no	no	$75	1 - 2 Months	yes	no
CO[9]	maybe	yes	maybe	no	no	$0	2 Months	yes	yes
CT	yes	yes	no	yes[10]	no	$0	3 Months	yes	yes
DC	No intrastate traffic to regulate.								
DE [11]	yes	yes	yes	no	no	$750	2 Months	yes	yes
FL [12]	yes	yes	no	no	no	$250	3 Months	yes	yes
GA	yes	yes	no [13]	no	no	$0	6 - 7 Months	yes [14]	no
HI	yes	yes	no	no	no	$30	1 Month	yes	yes
IA	Deregulated.								
ID	Registration	yes	no	no	no	$0	30 Days	yes	yes

State	Certification	Tariff	Cost Support	Attend Hearing	Attorney	Filing Fees	Time Estimate	Certificate of Foreign Corp[1]	Registered Agent[2]
IL	yes	yes	no	yes [15]	no	$0	3-4 Months	yes	no
IN	yes	no[16]	no	no	no	$0	5-6 Months	yes	yes
KS	Registration	yes	no	no	no	[17]	3 Months	yes	no
KY	Registration	yes	no	no	no	$0	30 Days	yes	yes
LA	yes	yes	no	no	no	$250	4 - 5 Months	yes	yes
MA	yes	yes	no	no	no	[18]	30 Days	no	no
MD [19]	yes	yes	no	no	no	$0	2 - 3 Months	yes	yes
ME [20]	yes	yes	no	no	no	$0	2 - 3 Months	yes	yes
MI	As of 10/97, not regulated and nothing pending. Informational tariff allowed.								
MN [21]	yes	yes	no	no	no	[22]	3 - 4 Months	yes	yes
MO	yes	yes	no	no	yes	$0	2 Months	yes	yes
MS	yes	yes	no	yes[23]	yes	$0 [24]	2 Months	yes	yes
MT	As of 6/97, resellers must register. Electronic registration form at **www.psc.mt.gov/tcom/register.htm**. A reseller can start providing service as soon as it receives verification of receipt of the filing. This is very quick and typically is 3 - 4 days at the most. Tariff not required.								
NC	yes[25]	no[26]	no	no[24]	no	$250	2 - 3 Months	yes	no
ND	Registration	no	no	no	no	$0	2 Months	yes	no

State	Certification	Tariff	Cost Support	Attend Hearing	Attorney	Filing Fees	Time Estimate	Certificate of Foreign Corp[1]	Registered Agent[2]
NE	yes	yes	no	yes[27]	no	$50	3 Months	yes	yes
NH	Registration	yes	no	no	no	$0	30 Days	yes	yes
NJ	Resellers must file Resale Acknowledgement Form with New Jersey Bell. As of 10/97 not regulated.								
NM[28]	yes	yes	no	no	maybe[29]	$250	4 Months	yes	no
NV[30]	yes	no	no	no	no	$200	6 Months	yes	no
NY	yes	yes	no	no	no	$0	3 Months	no	no
OH	Switchless resellers without CIC codes may file application for relief from jurisdiction. Takes about 30 days.								
OK[31]	yes	yes	no	no	no	$35	7-9 Months	yes	no
OR	yes	no	no	no	no	$0	2 Months	no	no
PA	yes	yes	no	no	no	$250	4 Months[32]	yes	yes
RI	Registration	yes	no	no	no	$250	30 Days	yes	yes
SC[33]	yes	yes	no	yes	recommend	$0	6 Months	yes	no
SD	yes	yes	no[34]	no	no	$250	3 Months	yes	yes
TN	yes	Price list[35]	no	no	no	$50	2-3 Months	yes	no
TX	Registration[36]	yes	no	no	no	$0	N/A	no	no

State	Certification	Tariff	Cost Support	Attend Hearing	Attorney	Filing Fees	Time Estimate	Certificate of Foreign Corp[1]	Registered Agent[2]
UT	As of 10/97, not regulated. No regulation pending.								
VA	As of 10/97, not regulated. No regulation pending.								
VT[37]	yes	yes	no	no	no	$0	6 Months	yes	yes
WA[38]	Registration	yes	no	no	no	$0	2-3 Months	no	yes
WI	yes	no	no	no	no	$250[39]	3 Months	yes	no
WV[40]	yes	yes	no	no	no	$0	6 Months	yes	no
WY	Registration	yes	no	no	no	$15	1 Day	yes	yes
FCC Interstate	no	yes[41]	no	no	no	$1,345 Min.[42]	1 Day	N/A	N/A
FCC Intl.	yes	yes	no	no	no	$1,345 Min.[42]	50 Days	N/A	N/A

Footnotes for Typical Requirements for 1+ Switchless Resellers by Jurisdiction

1   If your company is not incorporated but wants to do business in a state, a Certificate of Foreign Corporation is usually required. This column indicates if a copy of that certificate should be attached to your application for certification/registration.

2   This column indicates if the name and address of your registered agent must be included in your application for certification/registration.

3   There are three carriers authorized to provide service: Alascom, GCI, and Sprint (calling cards only). However, AT&T is in the process of acquiring Alascom. Newspaper notices are required.

4   The Attorney General's office sometimes intervenes in reseller applications. BellSouth can walk in the day of hearing to intervene. With intervention, we recommend using an attorney during the hearing.

5   Staff says that you can begin operating as soon as you have proof of filing.

6   While a copy is not required, you must sign a statement that you have received your certificate.

7   Must have $25,000 in unincumbered capital.

8   If exempt from tariffing requirements, must comply with the Consumer Protection Rules adopted in Decision 96-09-098.

9   Except for companies that resell non-optional operator services, resellers are not regulated. However, non-optional operator services include directory assistance and operator toll assistance. A waiver from regulation may be possible.

10 If no intervention, the hearing can be held by telephone.

11 Bond required for deposits. Notice must be published in newspapers.

12 Amendment to rule 25-4.0042 on 1/12/92 prohibits carriers to sell to resellers who are not certified in the State of Florida.

13 Must offer a service equal to or less than AT&T MTS and calling card service on a cell-by-cell comparison. All outbound services must offer 0-16 miles free.

14 Must include the "charter or file identification number" from your Certificate of Authority as a Foreign Corporation issued by the Secretary of State.

15 If there is no intervention, hearing may be conducted via telephone.

Footnotes for Typical Requirements for 1+ Switchless Resellers by Jurisdiction (continued)

16 A tariff is required if you resell operator services to traffic aggregators or operate as an AOS company.

17 Applicant will be billed for staff time. No estimate of cost at this time.

18 $15 plus $.15 per page of tariff beyond 30 pages.

19 Financials must be strong. Commission is rejecting companies with losses and/or negative equity.

20 Will grant waiver from double payment of access charges on switched services but not for dedicated service.

21 The commission has recently rejected resellers with weak financial statements. Debit cards may require bond.

22 No filing fee. However, applicant will be billed an hourly rate for the number of hours spent on the application. Typically runs $100 - $500.

23 Without intervention, hearing will probably be waived.

24 Commission will bill company for cost of publishing notice, which is about $50.

25 Debit cards are not regulated in North Carolina.

26 Switched-based resellers must file tariff and attend hearing.

27 Hearing fee of $50 per half day session. If videoconferencing is used, the commission will bill hearing fee and the reseller will pay the video fee. Must be paid before order is issued.

28 New rules effective 4/29/96 ask for audited monthly financial statements. May file internal financials without audit.

29 If staff is not satisfied with your financials, you will go to hearing and local attorney will be required.

30 Must have good financial statements and/or strong telecom experience.

31 Must publish notices in two newspapers on two consecutive weeks.

32 When you receive your letter from the commission accepting the filing, you may offer service.

33 Must publish legal notices in four newspapers.

Footnotes for Typical Requirements for 1+ Switchless Resellers by Jurisdiction (continued)

34   While not required with your application, may be required in response to data request. Must sell above cost.

35   The reseller is not required to maintain price list/tariff at the commission. However, reseller must be able to provide Commission a current price list within ten days of a request.

36   Must register in state within 30 days of beginning Texas operations.

37   Must publish notices in two newspapers.

38   A two-step process. A reseller must first file for registration. Then a petition must be filed for classification as a competitive telecommunications company. Staff taking close look at financial statements. Debit cards require bond.

39   Effective 12/1/97.

40   Must publish notice of filing in 19 newspapers designated by the PSC.

41   Proposed rule making would eliminate interstate tariffs.

42   Filing fee of $745 for the 214 petition. If you have mileage sensitive services or need to reference another tariff, a special permission petition must be filed with a fee of $600. Filing fee for each tariff filing is $600. The interstate and international tariffs may be filed together or separately.

FCC Time Line

Days to FCC Approval	Event	Event Description
50 - 45	File 214 Petition with FCC.	The 214 petition requests authority to provide international service.
40	Client provides rates on diskette. (Lotus 123 or Quatro Pro)	
39 - 28	Visiology develops interstate tariff.	
35	FCC publishes notice for 214 Authority.	The 214 petition is effective 35 days after notice unless there is intervention.
30 - 25	Client approves interstate tariff.	
24 - 18	Visiology develops international tariff.	
14	Client approves international tariff.	
10	File special permission petition.	A special permission petition is required to reference another tariff. If the client has mileage sensitive rates, a special permission petition will be required to reference the V & H coordinates. **Requires additional filing fee of $600.**
9-1	File interstate and international tariffs with FCC.	The tariffs may be effective on one day's notice. The international tariff may have an effective date on or after the effective date of the 214 petition.
0	Approval	

GLOSSARY

Asynchronous Transfer Mode (ATM). This is a high-speed transmission line that carries two-way voice, video, and data at super-high speed over a combination of copper and fiber. The current speed limit of 155 megabits per second will soon be exceeded by a 622 megabit version. ATM uses a form of packet switching, as the Internet does, that breaks information into packets of 53 bytes each. Five of the bytes are reserved for routing information. This allows packets from numerous different phone calls and data transmissions to share the same circuit without getting lost or interfering with each other. ATM can be used for public or private networks, like the Internet, but it has enough capacity for live, two-way, full-motion video. The U.S. Government is funding a wireless ATM system known as the Mobile Information Infrastructure Project. The idea is to create a nationwide wireless network that allows people to send and receive multimedia data with wireless laptop computers.

Asynchronous Digital Subscriber Line (ADSL). This allows transmission of digital video and data in one direction over a regular copper line at a relatively high speed of 1.5 megabits a second, which is on par with a TI line. Information from the network to the user moves much faster than information from the user back to the network. Hence, it's designation as an *asynchronous* system.

Audiotext (also Audiotex). This term broadly describes various telecommunications equipment and services that enable users to send or receive information by interacting with a voice processing system via a telephone connection, using audio input. Voice-mail, interactive 800 or 900 programs, and telephone banking transactions are examples of applications that fall under this generic category.

Automatic Number Identification (ANI). A means of identifying the telephone number of the party originating the telephone call, through the use of analog or digital signals that are transmitted along with the call and equipment that can decipher those signals.

Automated Attendant. A device, connected to a PBX, that performs simple voice processing functions limited to answering incoming calls and routing them in accordance with the touch-tone menu selections made by the caller.

Automatic Call Distributor (ACD). A specialized phone system used for handling a high volume of incoming calls. An ACD will answer an incoming call, then refer to its programming for instructions on what to do with that call. Based on these instructions, it will send the call to a recording giving the caller further instructions or to a voice response unit (VRU). It can also route the call to a live operator.

Call-Center. A facility staffed with numerous personnel who handle a high volume of either incoming or outgoing telephone calls, or both. Telemarketing operations are *outbound* call-centers. Customer service, technical support, or order-taking operations are *inbound* call-centers. The operators are typically networked with computers and specialized software and databases, which help them serve the callers as necessary, from processing orders to troubleshooting a technical problem (see Screen Pop).

Central Office. This is a local phone company building where all phone lines in the surrounding geographic area terminate. From this point the calls are *switched*, or routed, to another local phone connected to the same central office, to another central office serving a more distant area, or to the long-distance network.

Centrex. A central office-based service provided by the local phone company, which offers PBX-like enhanced services such as conference calling, call forwarding, call hold, intercom, and caller ID. These services turn simple single-line phones into a virtual phone system without incurring the expense of buying the hardware.

Coaxial cable. The thick copper cables used in the construction of traditional cable TV systems.

Code Division Multiple Access (CDMA). A wireless digital technology used by PCS providers. It carries up to ten conversations on a single channel. Analog cellular systems carry only one conversation per channel.

Competitive Access Provider (CAP). A carrier that provides a direct, discount link between companies and other major telephone customers and their long-distance carrier, bypassing the local carrier.

Competitive Local Exchange Carrier (CLEC). A carrier that provides full local service in competition with a dominant local phone company.

Computer Telephony. Also known as *Computer-Telephone Integration.* The convergence of computer and telecommunications technologies. Microchips and computers allow for all kinds of sophisticated automated capabilities to be added to the basic telephone. Fax-on-demand, interactive voice response, and videoconferencing are all the results of computer telephony.

Dial-Around. A method that allows callers to dial a code and use any long-distance service for a single call. Every long-distance carrier has a five-digit access code, with the first two digits always "1" and "0" (10XXX). This allows callers to use their preferred carrier from any location.

Dual Tone Multi-Frequency (DTMF). The technical term describing push button or touch-tone dialing. When you touch a button on a telephone keypad, it makes a tone, which is actually a combination of two tones—one high frequency and one low frequency. Hence the name Dual Tone Multi-Frequency.

Enhanced Services. Services provided by the telephone company over its network facilities, which may be provided without filing a tariff, usually involving some computer-related feature such as formatting data or restructuring the information. Also refers to optional services such as caller ID, call forwarding, call waiting, and voice-mail.

Ethernet. A local area network (LAN) that links computers and peripherals (printers, terminals) within one office or building. Either twisted copper telephone wire or coaxial cable can be used.

Extranet. A computer network consisting of more than one organization (see Intranet), such as an industry group or a supplier and its customers. Access is controlled to maintain the security of the network. Dedicated high-speed lines are usually leased from the phone company to link the sites together.

Fax Broadcasting. An automated system for broadcasting the same fax message to a large number of recipients.

Fax-On-Demand. An automated, computer-based system that allows a caller to select documents, usually from a menu of selections, to be transmitted back to his or her fax machine.

Fiber-Optic Cable. Consists of strands of glass filaments that transmit data using flashes of laser light. This is a relatively low-cost means of transmitting large amounts of data for long distances with little distortion. The "backbones" of most long-distance networks are built with fiber-optic cable. The first generation of commercial long-distance fiber-optic networks appeared in the 1980s. The technology has advanced since then. Older cables carried flashes of light at a single wavelength, or color. The newest cables have eight windows, or streams of light, operating with different colors. Each color stream within the fiber carries about 10 gigabits of information. The division of the cable into multiple lanes is achieved by a compression technique known as *wavelength division multiplexing*. It's still evolving. The next generation of fiber will have 16 windows, each capable of carrying 40 gigabits of information a second.

Frame Relay. This is a data service that operates at speeds up to 12.2 megabits a second. It was designed to carry just data, but it is carrying voice now as well. It creates something called a *virtual circuit*. Instead of creating an exclusive connection or circuit between two phone lines, frame relay systems create a defined path through a shared network.

Global Standard for Mobile Communications (GSM). GSM is a European wireless digital technology, the European version of TDMA. GSM phones also accept so-called smart cards, which can customize a single phone with such features as additional phone numbers, which allow the same phone to be used by different people.

High Speed Digital Subscriber Line (HDSL). This is similar to ADSL, turning regular copper wire into a high-speed circuit, but it sends information at high speed in both directions, at 6 megabits per second or faster. At faster speeds, it's suitable for live, two-way, video transmission.

Hub. A common collection or distribution point for multiple circuits in a network.

Incumbent Local Exchange Carrier (ILEC). This term was created as a result of the Telecommunications Act of 1996 to differentiate between the *established* local phone company and a new entrant into the market, which is known as a *competitive local exchange carrier* (CLEC).

Integrated Services Digital Network (ISDN). This is a data service that transmits digital information over a copper line at 128 kilobits a second. It's ten times faster than a 28.8 modem, which makes it adequate for retrieving text and some graphics and video from the Internet, but it isn't fast enough to support live video. Customers must buy special pieces of equipment that attach their computer modems to the phone line. They allow customers to make phone calls and receive faxes or data transmissions at the same time. Each ISDN line requires two modems: one in the network and one on the customer's computer. They cost several hundred dollars each, but the customer pays for only one of them.

Interactive. An audiotext capability that allows the caller to select options from a menu of programmed choices in order to control the flow of information. As the term implies, the caller truly interacts with the computer, following the program instructions and selecting the information he or she wishes to receive.

Interactive Voice Response (IVR). The telephone keypad substitutes for the computer keyboard, allowing anyone with a touch-tone telephone to interact with a computer. Instead of displaying information on a computer screen, IVR uses a digitized voice to convey the desired information to the caller, who follows the voice prompts and menu selections to get the desired results.

Interexchange Carrier (IXC). This term technically applies to carriers that provide telephone service between LATAs (see below). Long-distance companies such as AT&T, Sprint, and MCI are also known as interexchange carriers.

International Call-back. Used by businesses and travelers in foreign countries that have high international calling rates. Using a pre-assigned, dedicated phone number, you dial your call-back service, located in the states, and hang up after one ring. Because you hang up after only one ring, without actually completing the call, the local phone company cannot charge you for a completed call. However, that one ring is enough to signal the switch/computer that you called, seeking a dial tone to set up a call.

Recognizing your pre-assigned call-in number, the switch/computer is programmed to immediately dial you back at the phone number you previously designated, referred to as your *call-back number*. You now have a dial tone that originates in the U.S. Then you will be prompted by the switch/computer to enter the phone number you want to call. Once this is accomplished, the call is set up, consisting of two legs that both originate in the U.S: one to your location and another to the party you are calling.

Internet Protocol (IP). The protocol for routing traffic on the Internet. This is how your e-mail finds its intended destination. The technology that underlies the Internet, intranets, and extranets. Breaks data into tiny pieces known as packets, which share circuits with other transmissions. Each piece is coded so it doesn't get lost.

Internet Service Provider (ISP). An organization that offers access to the Internet, through a dial-up telephone modem connection, to its customers, usually for a fee. Independent businesses, online service providers, such as AOL, and phone companies offer this service.

Intranet. A computer network limited to one company or organization. It can be limited to one building or spread out across the country, using high-speed leased lines provided by the phone company. Access is carefully controlled, and the network is often protected by a *firewall*, which makes it difficult for hackers to gain access.

Local Access Transport Area (LATA). This is a geographic service area that generally conforms to standard metropolitan and statistical areas (SMSAs). Some 200 were created with the breakup of AT&T. The local telephone companies provide service within each LATA (Intra-LATA), while a long-distance carrier (IXC) must be used for service between LATAs (Inter-LATA).

Local Area Network (LAN). A network of linked computers and peripheral devices. Usually limited to individual homes, offices or buildings, or small geographic areas such as a campus or a commercial complex.

Local Exchange Carrier (LEC). This is the local telephone company that provides service within each LATA, including Regional Bell Operating Companies (RBOCs) and independent LECs such as General Telephone (GTE). There are also several hundred small independent LECs that serve less populated rural areas. The LEC handles all billing and collections within its LATA, often including long-distance charges (Inter-LATA), which are collected and forwarded to the appropriate interexchange carriers.

Local Multipoint Distribution Service (LMDS). A high-capacity wireless transmission system capable of carrying voice, video, and data. It operates at the 28 gigaherz frequency. The federal government plans to auction licenses covering the United States in 1998.

Modem (MOdulate/DEModulate). A device that translates digital messages from your computer into analog messages that can be sent over regular analog (POTS) phone lines. Another modem at the other end of the line will reconvert the message back into digital form so that the receiving computer can decipher the message.

Multi-channel Multi-point Distribution System (MMDS). The first attempt to develop a wireless video system was known as MMDS or, even more simply, as wireless cable. It has been used as an alternative to cable television. The analog version carries only 33 channels. MMDS is prone to interference and requires a clear line of sight.

Multiplex. To transmit more than one signal over a single circuit, by using special encoding and decoding equipment at each end of the transmission path.

Network Computer (NC). A low-cost, stripped-down PC with limited capabilities, essentially for connecting to a network, such as the Internet, and little else. Also called Internet Computers (ICs).

Node. A communications or computing device attached to a network, such as a PC or a server.

North American Numbering Plan. The method of identifying telephone trunks and assigning service access codes (area codes) in the public network of North America, also known as World Numbering Zone 1.

Online Call Detail Data (OCDD). Information summarizing inbound calling data, typically detailing call volumes originating from different telephone area codes or states. Useful for tracking response rates to regional advertising.

Operations Support Systems (OSS). Also known as Operating Support Systems; the computer programs that monitor and administer telecommunications networks.

Packet-Switching. A data transmission system that breaks data into little pieces that share transmission lines and are sent in brief bursts, minimizing the use of network resources. The pieces, known as packets, are coded so they don't get lost. It's more efficient than traditional phone systems, which reserve a separate circuit for the full duration of each call.

Pay-Per-Call. The caller pays a predetermined charge for accessing information services, at a rate in excess of the underlying transport charges. 900 numbers are one example of such a service. Pay-per-call services may also be offered over 800 or regular toll lines using credit cards or other third-party billing mechanisms. When the caller pays a premium above the regular transport charges for the information content of the program, regardless of how payment is made, it is considered a pay-per-call service.

Personal Communications Services (PCS). A new digital wireless cellular service over a new frequency spectrum recently auctioned off by the FCC. Offers superior digital communications for both voice and data. The FCC has licensed up to six PCS carriers in each market. PCS is similar to cellular, although it operates at 1900 megahertz, while cellular operates at 800 megahertz. PCS networks use smaller cells, which allow them to use lighter, longer-lasting batteries.

Personal Digital Assistant (PDA). Multifunction communications device that looks like a little palmtop computer, which may perform calendar, memo pad, calculator, and scheduling functions, as well as e-mail and paging.

Prepaid Debit Card. See Prepaid Phone Card.

Prepaid Phone Card. A card with a predetermined number of minutes or message units, normally used for long-distance calling. The card is tied to a prepaid phone card *platform*, which is essentially a computer that accepts the inbound call from the cardholder (usually via a toll-free 800 number), routes the outbound call to the desired party, keeps track of the message units consumed and remaining, and alerts the caller at certain intervals as the message units are depleted. Some prepaid phone cards also have a replenishment feature, where the cardholder can call into the system and buy additional message units with a credit card, using an IVR system to input all the data and to complete the transaction.

Port. In the context of telecommunications and computers, the interface between a computer or voice-processing system and a communications or transmission facility. For example, where you plug your computer into the phone line. The place where the physical connection is made between a computing device and a cable.

POTS. Plain Old Telephone Service. The basic analog service consisting of standard single-line telephones, telephone lines, and access to the public switched network.

Private Branch Exchange (PBX). PBX is a private telephone switching system (as opposed to public), usually located in an organization's premises, with an attendant console, or switchboard, which can be manual or automated. It is connected to a group of lines from one or more central offices to provide services to a number of individual phones, such as in a hotel, business, or government office.

PTT (Post Telephone & Telegraph administration). A generic term that refers to government-owned monopolies that control the telecommunications networks and services in most foreign countries.

Public Switched Telephone Network (PSTN). The worldwide telephone network, consisting of switched wireline and wireless services, including local exchange carriers, interexchange carriers, and wireless service providers. Accessible to anyone with a telephone who pays the required access charges.

Regional Bell Operating Company (RBOC). These are the seven holding companies that were created by the breakup of AT&T (also known as *Baby Bells*):

1. Nynex
2. Bell Atlantic
3. Ameritech
4. BellSouth
5. Southwestern Bell Corp. (SBC)
6. US West
7. Pacific Telesis

As of this writing, Nynex has merged with Bell Atlantic, and Pacific Telesis with Southwestern Bell. These companies own many of the various LECs; however, there are numerous independent LECs that are not owned by an RBOC, such as Southern New England Telephone (SNET) and GTE, two of the largest.

Resellers. Companies that purchase wholesale telephone services, such as long-distance, from facilities-based carriers and resell the services under their own names/brands. These companies range in size from small operations to billion-dollar companies, many with annual revenues exceeding $100 million. Although these companies started by selling long-distance service, many are now expanding into local service, wireless resale, paging, Internet access, calling cards, and other telecommunications services. Some of these companies may own their own switching systems and other network facilities (often referred to as *switched* resellers), but they still lease lines from other carriers to complete their coverage. Those that do not own any network facilities are called *switchless* resellers (see below).

Router. A device that connects multiple networks and manages the flow of data between them, such as finding the best route and establishing communications priorities.

Screen Pop. When a customer service representative, order taker, or any other person in a call-center fields an incoming call, the calling party's telephone number is often identified through caller ID or ANI, and then matched to the caller's record in the company's database. The caller's record is then automatically displayed (pops) on the computer screen, which may show name, address, order history, model number, sizes, or other preferences, helping the representative be as efficient as possible in helping the caller.

Service Bureau. A company that provides voice processing and audiotext equipment and services, and connection to telephone network facilities. These companies can offer a variety of communications services, such as fax-on-demand, fax broadcasting, international call-back, prepaid phone cards, IVR programs, 900 services, automated order processing, and other related services. An alternative to purchasing equipment and operating such services in-house.

Signaling System 7 (SS7). A network signaling system that improves network efficiency and allows for the provision of advanced services. For example, SS7 will exchange data with network databases and switches to determine the best possible transmission path for a voice call before the call is connected, which optimizes the use of network resources. SS7 also enables enhanced services such as call forwarding, caller ID, call blocking, and automatic call-back.

Switch. A computer on the phone network that connects one phone to another during a call. It assigns an open circuit and sends the call through it.

Switchless Reseller. Companies that do not own a switching system or any other network facilities, but purchase telephone services in large wholesale volume from facilities-based carriers or larger resellers at big discounts. These companies then sell to end-users under their own brand/name, performing all marketing, billing, and collection functions.

Synchronous Optical Network (SONET). Many local networks use fiber-optic transmission lines known as SONET rings. In addition to their enormous bandwidth capacity for carrying calls, they also have separate channels that carry information about the performance of the network. This allows the phone company to manage the network and to instantly reroute a call if the SONET ring is broken.

T-1 (also spelled T1). A digital transmission link with a capacity of 1.544 Mbps (1,544,000 bits per second). T-1 normally can handle 24 simultaneous voice conversations or data links over two pairs of wires, each one digitized at 64 Kbps. This is accomplished by using special encoding and decoding equipment at each end of the transmission path, which *multiplexes* one circuit into 24 channels. T-2, T-3, and T-4 (below) refer to links with increasingly higher capacities.

T-2. Four times the capacity of T-1 at 6.312 Mbps, capable of 96 voice conversations or data links.

T-3. Twenty-eight T-1 lines, or 44.736 Mbps, capable of 672 voice conversations or data links, carried on fiber-optic cable.

T-4. 168 times the capacity of T-1 at 274.176 Mbps, capable of handling 4032 voice conversations or data links.

Tariff. Documents filed by a regulated telephone company with a state public utility commission or the Federal Communications Commission. The tariff describes services, equipment, and pricing offered by the telephone company to all potential customers. As a "common carrier," the telephone company must offer its services to the general public at the prices and conditions outlined in its tariffs.

Telecard. See Prepaid Phone Card.

Time Division Multiple Access (TDMA). A wireless digital technology, used by PCS and digital cellular providers, which carries three to six conversations on a single channel. Analog cellular systems carry only one conversation per channel.

Time Division Multiplexing (TDM). A method for *multiplexing* one circuit into several channels, allowing the simultaneous transmission of numerous voice, data, or video signals over one circuit.

Trunk. A communication line between two switching systems. The term *switching systems* typically includes equipment in a central office (the telephone company) and PBXs. A *tie trunk* connects PBXs, while *central office trunks* connect a PBX to the switching system at the central office.

Videoconferencing. The PC-based desktop models of this equipment consist of a little video camera mounted on the monitor, a video card, speakers, and software to make it all work. The software may also support *document conferencing*, where both parties can work on the same document simultaneously, each seeing what the other changes on the document. This technology works best on higher-speed connections such as ISDN, because the performance on regular analog phone lines is fuzzy, jerky, and slow.

Voice-mail System. A computerized system that records, stores, and retrieves voice messages. You can program the system (voice mail boxes) to forward messages, leave messages for inbound callers, add comments and deliver messages to you, etc. It is essentially a sophisticated answering machine for a large business with multiple phone lines (probably with a PBX), or it can be a network-based service provided by the phone company.

Voice Processing. This is the general term encompassing the use of the telephone to communicate with a computer by way of the touch-tone keypad and synthesized voice response. Audiotex, speech recognition, and IVR are sub-classifications under voice processing.

Voice Recognition. Also known as *Speech Recognition.* The ability of a computer to recognize human speech and the spoken word.

Voice Response Unit (VRU). This is the building block of any voice-processing system, essentially a voice computer. Instead of a computer keyboard for entering information (commands), a VRU uses remote touch-tone telephones. See *Interactive Voice Response.*

Wave Division Multiplexing (WDM). A technique that divides a fiber-optic line into numerous channels, greatly increasing its capacity.

Wide Area Network (WAN). A geographically dispersed network of computers, connected with phone company high-speed data lines. Can consist of one company and its various global locations, a group of related businesses, or any grouping of organizations that need to share information quickly and reliably. The telephone network connections can be over the regular switched network or on dedicated lines leased from the phone company.

INDEX

About the Author

Steve Rosenbush is the telecommunications reporter at *USA Today*. He has written extensively about industry deregulation, the breakup of AT&T, and the rise of new companies challenging the industry order. Along the way, he has interviewed the major players in the telecom industry, from the CEOs at the giant telephone companies to the agile entrepreneurs at the high-tech start-up firms. He also worked as a business writer at the *Star-Ledger* in Newark and as an assignment editor on UPI's international business desk in New York. He resides in New York City with his wife and daughter.

Steve Rosenbush welcomes comments on this book. He can be reached at srosenbush@aegisbooks.com.